Speaking as a Professional

Speaking as a Professional

Enhance Your Therapy or Coaching Practice through Presentations, Workshops, and Seminars

Dan Grandstaff

W.W. Norton & Company

New York • London

For information about permission to reproduce
selections from this book, write to
Permissions, W. W. Norton & Company, Inc.
500 Fifth Avenue, New York, NY 10110

Composition and book design by Viewtistic, Inc.
Manufacturing by Quebecor World Fairfield Graphics
Production Manager: Leeann Graham

Library of Congress Cataloging-in-Publication Data
Grandstaff, Dan.
   Speaking as a professional: enhance your therapy or coaching practice through presentations,
workshops, and seminars/Dan Grandstaff.
      p.   cm.
   "A Norton professional book."
   Includes bibliographical references and index.
   ISBN 0-393-70433-5
   1. Public speaking. I. Title.

PN4129.15.G73   2004
808.5'1—dc22   2004046530

W. W. Norton & Company, Inc., 500 Fifth Avenue, New York, NY 10110
www.wwnorton.com
W. W. Norton & Company, Ltd., Castle House, 75/76 Wells Street, London W1T 3QT
1 2 3 4 5 6 7 8 9 0

I dedicate this book to my clients who have
inspired and taught me far more
than they can ever know.

Contents

List of Tables
and Worksheets

TABLES

WORKSHEETS

Acknowledgments

EVEN THOUGH MY NAME is on the cover of this book, many people have contributed their ideas, experiences, and support to make it a much better book than it could have been without them.

I gladly express my gratitude and appreciation to:

Judy Griffin who first encouraged me to write the guide that became this book and to Ann Loomis who inspired me by first writing her own book on writing.

All the members of my Natural Speaking workshops who taught me so much about facing fear and speaking naturally.

The members of my audiences, especially the congregations I served, whose caring and forgiving natures helped me realize I had something worth saying.

Deborah Malmud, my editor at W. W. Norton, who guided me patiently and expertly through the editing process. She taught me to write better, saved me from countless mistakes, and, even in the process of telling me what I was doing wrong, somehow managed never to hurt my feelings.

Michael J. McGandy, Associate Managing Editor at Norton, who handled the details of this project with efficiency, aplomb, and kindness.

Muriel Jorgenson, whose expert and careful copy editing made me much better looking, at least in print, and easier to read than I have ever been.

Andrea Costella, assistant editor at Norton, who handled so many details with good humor and grace.

Many therapists and coaches who generously shared their experiences as speakers. Even though they may not be quoted by name in the book, their contributions were significant: John Amodeo, Mark Brown, Jeff Davidson, Carol Eckerman, Bruce Etringer, Gail Finger, Chris Gellings, Laura Howard, Carol Jung, Victoria Leo, Donald Meichenbaum, Rebecca Merrill, William Meyer, Patti Prendergast, Bonnie Raphael, Lynn Skidmore, David Steffens, Marianna Thomas, Mary Beth Tobin, Debra Vajcner, Russell White, Elinor Williams, Jay Williams, and Reid Wilson.

Herb and Sharon Klein, Thomas Leonard, and Sandy Vilas for encouraging me with their positive feedback about my original guide.

Daphne Rosenblitt for such skilled patience in helping me find more of my voice and my self.

My parents, Paul and Mary, for encouraging me to find a way with words; Pat Grandstaff and my son, Peter Grandstaff, for being understanding about the time I spent writing and thinking about writing; and my partner, Carolyn, who generously gave me guilt-free time to write and who helps make each day an enjoyable and memorable adventure, no matter what I am doing.

Preface

THIS IS A BOOK FOR psychotherapists and coaches about how to use speeches, workshops, seminars, and presentations to enhance their practices and careers. Consultants, trainers, accountants, financial planners, attorneys, architects, dentists, chiropractors, and other health care professionals can also use these methods quite successfully and could easily adapt the approaches to their own situations. But the book is directed to and designed especially for coaches and psychotherapists.

The term *coach* includes personal coaches, life coaches, business coaches, career coaches, and the many subspecialties of these main coaching areas. The term *psychotherapist* includes psychologists, psychiatrists, clinical social workers, marriage and family therapists, licensed professional counselors, psychiatric nurses, clinical nurse specialists, and other subspecialties such as career counselors, bioenergetic therapists, and grief counselors. Although I use the term *practice* for the work that coaches and psychotherapists do, I also use the term *practice* for the work of agencies and counseling centers. Presentations and workshops can be powerful tools for promoting programs and institutions as well as individual private practices, and I have included examples to fit as many situations as possible.

Although psychotherapists and coaches have much in common, their needs and issues sometimes differ. I have tried to account for these divergences as much as possible by giving alternative examples and scenarios when needed for coaches and therapists.

Coaches should not automatically skip over examples for psychotherapists, however, and psychotherapists should not pass over the sections for coaches. Instead, think about how you can apply the suggested methods and examples to your own situation.

Since the terms *speech, presentation, workshop, seminar,* and *public speaking,* mean different things to different people, this is how I use the terms in this book. *Public speaking* and *presentation* are inclusive terms that cover almost any situation where you talk to a group of people. I will use these terms interchangeably in this book. A *speech* is a presentation, typically up to 60 minutes long, that usually does not include audience activities or extensive discussion during the speech. In common usage, a *presentation* is more likely than a speech to include audiovisual aids such as PowerPoint, although there are certainly exceptions. Seminars and workshops are both educational in nature, with workshops usually more focused on teaching and learning skills, whereas seminars more often focus on content other than skills. Workshops usually include more audience-participation activities (in addition to group discussion) than seminars. A teleclass or teleconference is a workshop or seminar conducted by telephone, with all the participants calling into a central number, called a bridge.

Speaking as a Professional follows a logical sequence, starting with an overview in Chapter 1, then moving through the steps you will need to follow to plan, prepare, and give presentations. In Chapter 2, you will identify and assess your strengths as a speaker as well as look at ways you can keep improving. In Chapter 3, you will learn what makes a good topic and title for a presentation, and how to decide what you want to talk about. Chapter 4 teaches you how to identify and contact groups that will be the audiences for your presentations. In Chapter 5, you will learn how to plan, prepare, and practice presentations. Chapter 6 teaches you what you need to know to be truly effective when you stand in front of your audience and speak. In Chapter 7, you will learn methods for managing fear and overcoming stage fright. Chapter 8 teaches you methods to keep your presentation working for you beyond the event itself, including how to follow up with members of the audience. Chapter 9 explains how to generate publicity for your presentations. In Chapter 10, you will learn the ins and outs of workshops, seminars, and training, including the keys to leading successful teleclasses and teleconferences. Chapter 11 gives advice and tips for improving academic and medical presentations. The Resources section provides an extensive list of books, tapes, Web sites, coaches, and classes you can use to keep growing as a speaker.

You will also find Exercises and Worksheets throughout the book. You will get the most value from this book from doing the Exercises as well as reading about them. Consider this book a workshop on using presentations to enhance your practice and career. The Exercises and Worksheets will be an essential part of your learning.

Dan Grandstaff
Chapel Hill, NC
dan@winwithpeople.com

CHAPTER 1

Speaking to Enhance Your Professional Practice and Career

DO YOU WANT TO attract more clients to your psychotherapy or coaching practice?

Would you like to be among the first professionals others think of when they are asked for a referral in your specialty?

Do you want to develop a new specialty or work with different kinds of clients than you do now?

Would you like to develop additional income sources besides working directly with coaching or therapy clients?

Are you interested in promoting a new service, program, organization, or product such as a book or tape series?

Would you like to become better known in your field to enhance your career or for the personal satisfaction of being publicly recognized for your work?

Do you wish you could help more people than you can reach through one-on-one or small-group therapy or coaching?

❏ WHY PUBLIC SPEAKING?

You could probably achieve many of these results by building your reputation slowly, sending out letters of introduction, attending professional meetings where you introduce yourself to professional colleagues, doing excellent work with each client you work with, and sending thank-you and follow-up notes to each person who makes a referral. But for most people, it would take several years to build a reputation among your peers this way. Even then, you would be known only to a small group of colleagues, usually within your own professional discipline and community. You would not stand out from the many other competent therapists and coaches in the community except for the personal relationships and impressions you developed with the people you met.

You can build your reputation and your practice much more quickly and effectively by giving presentations to groups of colleagues, prospective clients, and people who may recommend you to others. Through public speaking, you can make others aware of who you are and your niches, specialties, services, programs, organizations, or products. Through presentations and the resulting media exposure, you can reach and become known by many *more* people than you could reach through traditional networking.

Even if you are not concerned with quick results, giving speeches, presentations, and workshops are among the most *effective* ways for you as a therapist or coach to:

- Attract more clients
- Receive more referrals
- Develop new client niches
- Enhance your reputation in your community and your profession
- Expand your professional network
- Add or increase income streams
- Promote products, services, or programs
- Increase personal satisfaction by helping more people
- Educate people about an issue or topic
- Contribute your expertise to the community

Why is speaking such an effective way to achieve results like these? Read on for an overview of the advantages of giving presentations.

❏ ADVANTAGES OF GIVING PRESENTATIONS

You are talking to a group of prospective clients and referral sources. Almost any audience will have one or more people who could refer someone to you. Even if there are no prospective clients in the audience, they may tell friends, coworkers, neighbors, and family members about your presentation. You can learn to choose groups so that the audience will consist of a high percentage of prospective clients for your services or of people in a position to refer those who need your services.

You are speaking to anywhere from 5 to 500 people or more, all at once. How long would it take you to call on 40 or 50 people or to meet them at networking events? At least 40 hours if you call on them in person one at a time? At least 15 to 20 hours if you called and introduced yourself by phone? At least five or six gatherings if you met them at professional meetings? In a speech, you can do this in as little as an hour, with many other benefits you cannot get in other settings.

Your audience wants to hear what you have to say. The people in your audience are usually looking forward to hearing you speak. They are there to learn something new or to get a new perspective on a problem. You can learn how to choose topics and give presentations that speak to the burning problems of your audiences and prospective clients, making them almost guaranteed to be interested in your presentation.

You are educating and helping your audience with a problem. One of the most powerful stances to take as a speaker is that of teacher or educator. You give your audience new information and ways to think about problems. You tell them about solutions and approaches that have helped other people. You show them, indirectly, that you are knowledgeable and competent. And you give them tools they can use to understand or solve a problem.

Your audience is not resisting what you are saying because you are not "selling." Everyone's resistance goes up when someone is trying to sell them something. That is why you should never try to sell anything in a speech or presentation. You do not have to. Your audience is interested in what you have to say. And some of them will be interested in the services you provide.

Your audience will see you as an expert. Most people assume that if you are giving the program, you must know what you are talking about. You do not have to know everything there is to know about the topic. You will need to know enough more than the audience to talk about the topic in a reasonably coherent, informative, and interesting way. If you do, you will be considered an expert by the end of the presentation. People generally value and trust those whom they consider to be experts, especially if the "expert" is approachable and down to earth.

Your audience will appreciate you for being willing to speak to their organization. With many professional and civic organizations, you will not be paid for speaking. The members appreciate people who are willing to give helpful presentations. Even when you are paid to give a speech, people appreciate that you are willing to help them think about the problems and issues you are addressing. You start out with points on your scorecard with anyone from that organization.

Your audience will get to see you in person so that you are no longer an unknown. People buy services from people they know, like, and trust (or on the recommendation of someone they know, like, and trust). Often people buy needed services from the first person they meet who provides those services. When you give a speech, your audience not only finds out about you, but they get to see what you are like.

Your audience will get to talk with you directly. Not only will your audience get to see you, but they will have an opportunity to talk to you and ask you questions. In this way, giving a speech in person is even better than being on television. If the audience can ask you questions, they can get to know, like, and trust you more. You can engage them in conversation and build the kind of rapport that may lead to their calling you or your being able to follow up with them.

Your audience will have your name and contact information in a form that many will save or give to others. In many presentations to groups, it will not be appropriate to pass out business cards or brochures to all the members of the audience. Without a reminder, many people will forget you and your name within a day or so. It is almost always appropriate, however, for you to distribute a printed handout that relates to your presentation and contains your name, phone number, and other appropriate contact information.

Your audience may welcome additional follow-up if you offer more information in the form of a report or article. If an audience includes good prospects for your services, one way to encourage those prospects to identify themselves is to offer a report or article that supplements or elaborates on the subject of your presentation. This should be educational, not promotional. By offering to send the report or article to anyone who is interested, you add to your status as a helpful expert and get people to "raise their hands" to say they are interested in more information about your topic.

Your audience may include people of influence whom you would find difficult to meet otherwise. Many business and civic groups include presidents and CEOs of local companies and influential "gatekeepers" whom others listen to and respect. If you tried to call on them directly, you might find it difficult to get an appointment. But as a speaker, you may get to know them on a first-name basis. You may even find them wanting a chance to talk with you further.

Public speaking can enhance your exposure and reputation in your field, community, or profession. When you speak, you are automatically viewed as an expert by the audience, but speaking can also enhance your reputation among people who do not attend your speech, including colleagues. When people see your name in publicity or newspaper articles about the speech, they will identify you as an expert. When other people learn that you have been invited to speak on a particular topic, they may ask you to speak to another organization or company. The enhanced status that speaking brings can also lead to opportunities to write articles or columns, appear on panels, or be interviewed on radio and television, all of which can further enhance your standing and exposure.

Public speaking can lead to other income opportunities. In addition to attracting clients for your practice or organization, public speaking can lead to paid speeches, training, or seminars, as well as book and tape sales. Even though the primary focus of this book is how to enhance your coaching or therapy practice, public speaking can be lucrative for anyone willing to do what it takes to become a compelling speaker.

Noncelebrity paid speakers can earn up to $5,000 per speech, or even more. People who can translate their speaking into training can earn from $800 to $4,000 per day. And speakers can increase their earnings even more by putting their talks on audio- or videotapes or by producing books or training manuals that can be offered for sale after a speech.

❑ CONCERNS ABOUT PUBLIC SPEAKING

Since you are reading this book, you must have some interest in and curiosity about the potential of public speaking as a tool for enhancing your practice. But you may also have some doubts and misconceptions. Here are some common objections that people express about speaking as a way to enhance their practices.

Objection: I'm not comfortable speaking to large groups.

Response: You do not need to speak to large groups. In the beginning, you may focus on speaking to small groups of 3 to 12 people. Furthermore, if you are uncomfortable speaking to groups, you have probably been avoiding it. To make the most of speaking as a tool, then, you will need to practice your speaking skills in small groups before you consider speaking to a larger group. If you are not comfortable with your speaking skills, you may choose to take a speaking workshop, attend Toastmasters, or work with a speaking coach before giving talks to other groups. As you practice and learn methods for dealing with your discomfort and increasing your effectiveness, you will be able to expand your comfort zone to include larger groups.

Objection: I'm reasonably comfortable in front of groups, but I am not an entertaining or dynamic speaker.

Response: You do not have to be as funny as Robin Williams or as dynamic as Zig Ziglar to use public speaking as a marketing tool. You need to present your information and point of view in an "interesting" way. Pick a topic that interests you and has relevance for your audience. Aim to be clear, easy to follow, well organized, and reasonably lively. Do not belabor your points or use generalities. Use specific examples and memorable images. By the time you finish this book, you will know how to do all of these things. Your overall goal will probably be to let people know about you and to experience you as knowledgeable, trustworthy, and approachable. You can best do that by being yourself and using your unique speaking style.

Objection: I don't have time to prepare speeches all the time.

Response: Prepare one or two basic presentations that can be adapted to many audiences, but which will require little additional preparation after the first few times you give them. When you offer to speak, you should propose to speak on one of your prepared topics. (You can change the title to fit the audience without having to change the talk much at all.) You will also learn to prepare your presentation in *modules* so that you can add and rearrange sections to fit each audience. With some audiences and topics, you may give a brief presentation and spend most of the allotted time answering questions. These are a few ways to customize a presentation fairly quickly.

Objection: I'm not enough of an expert to give speeches and presentations.

Response: Whatever your field, you know more than most people who are not in your field or specialty. That makes you an expert. You know details and complexities of certain subjects or situations that other people want to know about. You have experiences and stories that people inside and outside your own field would be interested in, especially if you tell them in a slightly entertaining way. In addition, you probably have the ability to relate your knowledge to events taking place in the world. If you are a therapist, you are (or could easily become) more of an expert than most audiences on "Stress and Dual-Career Marriages," "Stress and Information Overload," "Grief and Everyday Losses," "The Power of Listening," "What Women and Men Could Learn From One Another," or other similar topics that could make good speeches. If you are a coach, you probably know enough to give a presentation on such topics as "The Importance of Value-Based Goals for True Success," "How to Make Great Decisions," "Creating Balance in Your Life," "Dealing With Difficult People at Work," and "What You Need to Know to Deal With Change and Transition."

Objection: I've done some public speaking and did not get a single referral.

Response: Not every speech will generate new clients, but most speeches will if you, as the speaker, follow guidelines such as these:

- Make sure the audience includes people who are prospective clients or referral sources.
- Speak on a topic that is a concern for your audience and that your services address in some way.
- Show that you understand and empathize with the challenges your audience faces, while also conveying a sense of hope about how the problems can be made better.
- Give a clear and interesting presentation as well as show an interest in the audience.
- Offer your audience an informative handout that includes your name and contact information.
- Provide an opportunity for interested audience members to speak with you afterward about specific questions they have.
- Make it easy for interested people to follow up for more information or an initial consultation.

In the next chapter we will explore the goals and outcomes *you* want from your speaking, identify and assess your strengths as well as areas you want to strengthen, and describe ways to improve and keep improving as a speaker.

CHAPTER 2

Discovering and Developing Your Strengths as a Speaker

WHEN PEOPLE JOIN A health club or spa, they may meet with a personal fitness trainer to talk about what they want to get out of their exercise program and to assess their current level of strength and fitness. Then they can design an exercise program that fits their needs and helps them move toward their goals. This chapter is intended to offer a similar kind of assessment and goal clarification process for you in your speaking.

What you focus on in developing as a speaker will depend on the outcomes you want to achieve, just as people primarily interested in developing aerobic capacity tailor their workouts accordingly. What you decide to do to develop your strengths as a speaker will depend on your current levels of experience and competence.

❏ IDENTIFYING YOUR GOALS

Until now you may not have thought about what you want to achieve with your speaking. The following exercises can help you start to clarify your goals and aspirations as a speaker.

EXERCISE 2.1 Goals for Public Speaking

This exercise can help you decide what you want to happen as a result of your speaking and the direction you want to take with your speaking.

Rate each of the following statements using the following scale: A = Key result you want from speaking. B = Secondary outcome, but not a main one. C = Not particularly important. Put a question mark next to any statements you are not sure about.

_____   You want to improve your skills in public speaking and presentations.

_____   You want to speak because you enjoy it.

_____   You want to do presentations because they are a challenge for you.

_____   You want to educate people about an issue or topic.

_____   You want to increase your referrals and clients.

_____   You want to attract other types of client or develop a new client niche.

_____   You want to expand your professional network.

_____   You want to enhance your reputation in your organization, community, or profession.

_____   You want to promote a service, program, or product.

_____   You want to do speaking or training as a new or larger source of income.

_____   Other: _____

_____   Other: _____

Look at the statements you have marked with an A. What patterns do you see about the key results you want from your speaking? Is your interest primarily for self-improvement, enjoyment, career development, outreach to the community, becoming better known, building your practice, increasing your income, promoting a program or product, or a combination of these? To help you identify the patterns, do the next exercise.

EXERCISE 2.2 Possible Results from Public Speaking

The same list of possible results appears below. Using a total of 100%, assess how important each outcome is to you by putting the percentage of emphasis you would place on each outcome.

In the following example, the person's primary interests are in building his or her practice and attracting other types of clients. The person also has some interest in educating people about an issue or topic and doing speaking or training as a source of income in itself.

Example:

_____ You want to improve your skills in public speaking and presentations.

_____ You want to speak because you enjoy it.

_____ You want to do presentations because they are a challenge for you.

_10_ You want to educate people about an issue or topic.

_40_ You want to increase your referrals and clients.

_40_ You want to attract other types of client or develop a new client niche.

_____ You want to expand your professional network.

_____ You want to enhance your reputation in your organization, community, or profession.

_____ You want to promote a service, program, or product.

_10_ You want to do speaking or training as a new or larger source of income.

_____ Other: _____

_____ Other: _____

Now it is your turn:

_____ You want to improve your skills in public speaking and presentations.

_____ You want to speak because you enjoy it.

_____ You want to do presentations because they are a challenge for you.

_____ You want to educate people about an issue or topic.

_____ You want to increase your referrals and clients.

_____ You want to attract other types of client or develop a new client niche.

_____ You want to expand your professional network.

_____   You want to enhance your reputation in your organization, community, or profession.

_____   You want to promote a service, program, or product.

_____   You want to do speaking or training as a new or larger source of income.

_____   Other: _____

_____   Other: _____

EXERCISE 2.3. Your Desired Results

Now, write a series of statements in your own words, either here or on a separate sheet of paper, about what you want as a result of speaking. What is it about speaking that interests you? What goals, however tentative, would you like to set for yourself and your speaking? Do not worry if you have only a vague idea now about what you want; this process is a first step that will become clearer as you work your way through the book.

_____

_____

_____

_____

_____

_____

Example (this fits with the percentages of the previous example):

I want to use speaking and seminars to attract more private pay clients.

I want to use speaking and seminars to become known as the therapist (or coach) who is an expert in helping people with weight loss through education, healthy personal awareness, and lifestyle changes.

I want to develop my reputation with physicians, therapists, and coaches who do not have the expertise or focus in this area.

I want to develop a series of paid workshops and programs as part of my approach.

You may not be this clear and focused yet. Write as much as you can about what you want or are thinking about.

❏ IDENTIFYING YOUR STRENGTHS

Now we will help you identify some of your strengths as a speaker. As you will see, you have strengths that can help you with your speaking even if you have not done any speaking.

EXERCISE 2.4. What You Know About

Brainstorm and write out two lists of subjects that you know about, (a) areas of theoretical and applied professional knowledge and (b) knowledge based on personal and life experiences. To qualify as an area of *professional* knowledge for your list, the subject should be one you could describe or explain for at least five minutes to a beginning professional student or client in your discipline. To qualify as knowledge based on personal and life experience, the subject should be one that you could talk about and tell stories about for at least five minutes in a one-on-one conversation. Include broad categories as well as specific areas of knowledge within the broad categories.

The purpose of this exercise is for you to discover how much you know at enough depth to talk about for five minutes. If you know this much, and are interested enough to do more research, you could talk about this topic with an audience of lay persons. (Some of the subjects will be areas you could talk about with a professional audience. We will discuss how to choose topics in the next chapter.) This exercise may give you ideas you would not have thought of otherwise. The main point of the exercise, however, is to show you areas of strength—professional and personal knowledge. The distinction between professional and personal knowledge is somewhat arbitrary and overlapping. What is important is that you *not* limit yourself in this exercise only to those areas that you have studied and know in depth.

As an example, here is my list:

Professional knowledge: presentation skills, cause and treatment of anxiety, cause and treatment of depression, dynamics of anger, dynamics of grief, human development over the lifespan, the psychotherapy process, family and relationship dynamics, marriage counseling process, human sexuality, the importance of boundaries, communication process, personality type, organizational development, conflict management, creative process, marketing, customer service, selection and hiring of employees.

Personal knowledge from experience: parenting and being a father, having a grown son, experience of a long marriage, experience of divorce, growing up in a family business, what it is like to be a minister, going back to graduate school after years of working, the value of community, committee meetings, experiencing the suicide of a friend, grief and loss, having aging parents, midlife love, being self-employed, writing and writer's block, procrastination, sibling relationships, adopted children, early and frequent user of computers and the Internet, having and being a neighbor, having and being a friend, English country dancing, learning to waltz in middle age, importance of grandparents, being in the hospital, successful and unsuccessful dieting, quitting smoking, how to exercise, meditation, satisfaction of home repairs, the healing power of nature and beauty, the joys and discomforts of travel, and more.

Now make your own list of professional and personal knowledge of which you have more than passing knowledge, experience, and interest. Keep the list handy and add to it over the course of a day or more. When you complete it, savor how much you know about, at least at this level. As professionals we are often quite aware of what we do *not* know. This is a chance to focus on and remember what you *do* know.

EXERCISE 2.5. People Who Affected You

Write down the names of everyone who has had an effect on you over the course of your life. If you do not remember or know people's names, identify them in some other way, such as "my first grade teacher" or "the person who took me to the ER after my accident." Try to list at least 50 people. The only criterion is that you remember their having an impact on you. Otherwise you would have forgotten about them. The point of this exercise is to realize how much more experience you have than you are usually aware of. Some of these people and their effect on you might be used eventually as an example or illustration in a presentation. One speaker described the difference that caregivers made when her husband died. Even though there were many people whose names she did not know, their caring made a difference. She used her list of people to develop a presentation on the difference that caregivers can make. Later, when you are planning and preparing your own presentations, refer to your list for examples. If I were doing a presentation on how to be a better boss, I would go to my list of bosses I have had, mostly good, and I would probably use one or two examples before asking the audience to remember their own first and best bosses. For now, let the list remind you of how rich and full your experiences have been. These are part of one of your strengths.

EXERCISE 2.6. Your Strengths as a Person and a Speaker

Circle (or write on a sheet of paper) the adjectives in the following list that describe you. Add other adjectives that you or others would see as your strengths or characteristics:

Easygoing	Energetic	Sincere	Factual
Down-to-earth	Inspiring	Funny	Prepared
Believable	Outspoken	Honest	Persuasive
Organized	Likeable	Trustworthy	Informed
Interested	Open	Sincere	Strong
Relaxed	Excited	Concerned	Logical
Friendly	Serious	Warm	Forceful
Creative	Imaginative	Modest	Optimistic
Trusting	Reflective	Patient	Calm
Intense	Tactful	Confident	Precise
Systematic	Original		

Write or say to yourself the following sentence, inserting all of the adjectives you chose: "By being myself, I can be a _____, _____, _____, _____, _____, _____, _____, and _____ speaker or workshop leader." Remove any adjectives that you feel do not fit. Add others that you may have overlooked. You may still find it hard to believe that you can be a speaker with these strengths, but if these are characteristics of you as a person, they are also characteristics of who you can be as a speaker. Write the completed sentence on an index card and refer to it regularly. This will help you affirm and appreciate the kind of speaker you are and can become.

EXERCISE 2.7. Assessing Areas for Strengthening

Identifying your strengths does not mean that you do not also have areas for improvement and strengthening. In the following section, you will identify your levels of experience, confidence, content, effectiveness, connections, and commitment related to giving speeches, presentations, and workshops. These exercises can help you decide where to focus your attention to strengthen the areas that are not strong now.

Experience

How much experience do you have doing presentations? What kinds of experience do you have—informal presentations, workshops, seminars, conference presentations, after-dinner speeches?

TABLE 2.1 LEVEL OF EXPERIENCE AT GIVING PRESENTATIONS

Level of experience	Description
5—Very High	You have given at least 5 presentations to the kinds of audiences you would like to speak to.
4—High	You have given at least 5 presentations, but to different kinds of audiences than you want to speak to.
3—Moderate	You have given at least 5 presentations, but not the type of presentations you want to give (for example, workshops or seminars instead of speeches, or speeches instead of workshops)
2—Low	You have given fewer than 5 presentations as a professional.
1—Very Low	You have almost no experience giving presentations.

If your level of experience is 2 or below, look for ways to get basic speaking experience. Where can you volunteer to give committee reports, make announcements, or give class presentations? How can you help lead a workshop or seminar, working with a more experienced leader? Are you part of a low-threat group where you could give a basic presentation or present a case? Chapter 4 describes how to get invited to give talks and gain necessary experience.

If your experience level is 3, consider where you can give the type of presentation you want to give but lack experience in presenting. If your effectiveness and confidence are low, work on those areas in a low-threat setting before trying to broaden your experience.

Effectiveness

How effective are your presentations? What do you need to improve?

TABLE 2.2 EFFECTIVENESS OF YOUR PRESENTATIONS

Level of effectiveness	Description
5—Very High	You have received very positive feedback from the presentations you have given.
4—High	You have received mostly positive feedback from the presentations you have given.
3—Moderate	You received average or mixed feedback from the presentations you have given.
2—Low	You have received feedback that your recent presentations were not very effective.
1—Uncertain	You have not given enough presentations in the past year to assess their effectiveness.

If your effectiveness level is 4 or 5, keep looking for new speaking experiences and keep doing what you have been doing; at the same time, always look for ways to improve. If your effectiveness level is 2 or 3, use the methods and resources throughout this book to identify what you most need to improve; focus on those areas. Focus on improving your effectiveness before seeking out challenging and significant speaking opportunities.

Confidence

How confident are you about your speaking? How well do you manage any fear or anxiety about speaking?

TABLE 2.3 CONFIDENCE ABOUT YOUR PUBLIC SPEAKING

Level of confidence	Description
5—Very High	You enjoy speaking and look forward to it. You are able to view any nervousness you feel as excitement.
4—High	You experience nervousness before you speak but it does not significantly interfere with your preparation and it mostly recedes once you start speaking.
3—Moderate	You get fairly nervous as you anticipate speaking. You are able to get through it, but it keeps you from being yourself in front of the audience.

TABLE 2.3 *Continued*

Level of confidence	Description
2—Low	You experience a great deal of anxiety before you speak that often interferes with your preparation. You either block in your preparation or overprepare in a way that decreases your effectiveness and enjoyment.
1—Very Low	You get so nervous that you mostly avoid speaking in front of groups (or the few times you have spoken you have been very nervous).

If your confidence level is 4 or 5, you can learn from the methods and techniques for managing your fear later in this book, but you probably do not need much help in this area. If your confidence level is a 3, you may be able to apply the fear-managing techniques on your own. If your confidence level is 2 or 1, try applying on your own the fear-managing techniques in Chapter 7, but also consider taking a class, joining Toastmasters, or working with a speaking coach. You can get considerable relief from your stage fright with the right help and support.

Content

How much content do you already have that you can use in presentations?

TABLE 2.4 CONTENT AVAILABLE FOR PRESENTATIONS

Level of content	Description
5—Very High	You already have at least one presentation or workshop prepared on a topic you want to speak on.
4—High	You know enough about one or more topics that you could speak for 30 minutes to a nonthreatening audience with less than 3 hours of preparation.
3—Moderate	You would need to do at least 4 hours of research to gather enough content for a speech you would want to give (the actual preparation of the presentation may take longer).
2—Low	You would need more than a half day of research to gather enough content for a speech you would want to give.
1—Very Low	You would need to start from the scratch in developing content for a presentation or workshop.

This book will walk you through the process of choosing a topic and preparing a presentation. If you do the research as you go along, you will have a presentation prepared by the time you finish the book.

Connections

How much of a network of connections do you have among the kinds of people you may want to speak to? Do you have a mailing list of organizations or know where you can obtain one?

TABLE 2.5 CONNECTIONS FOR SPEAKING ENGAGEMENTS

Level of connections	Description
5—Very High	You know and are known by leaders in several community or professional organizations that use speakers. You know at least 6 people who might be interested in having you speak to their organization.
4—High	You know several people who know people in organizations that use speakers, and you could approach people you know to get the names of good contacts in community or professional organizations.
3—Moderate	You know at least 2 people who would be good contacts for community or professional organizations that might be interested in having you as a speaker.
2—Low	You do not know people in community or professional organizations, but you can ask colleagues, neighbors, friends, or librarians to get a list of initial contacts.
1—Very Low	You do not know people in community or professional organizations, and you do not have any idea how you could make those contacts.

Lack of connections is an easy area to overcome if you are willing to make phone calls and meet with people in your community. If you are new to a community, offering to give presentations is one of the quickest ways to become known and get to know others. Refer to Chapter 4 for suggestions about networking and making connections in your community.

Time Commitment

How much time and interest do you have for giving presentations, workshops, or seminars? Are you willing and able to devote a few hours each week to developing presentations, refining your speaking skills, and seeking out possible audiences? Or will speaking be an activity that you fit into your schedule, if there is time?

TABLE 2.6 AMOUNT OF TIME YOU HAVE FOR PRESENTATIONS

Level of time commitment	Description
5—Very High	You are willing and able to spend at least 8 hours per week developing and giving presentations and workshops.
4—High	You are willing and able to spend 4 to 8 hours per week developing and giving presentations and workshops.
3—Moderate	You are willing and able to spend 2 to 4 hours per week developing and giving presentations and workshops.
2—Low	You are willing and able to spend 1 to 2 hours per week developing and giving presentations and workshops.
1—Very Low	You are not ready to commit time to preparing and giving presentations and workshops.

This scale is primarily a way for you to assess how much time and interest you have for doing presentations or workshops. If your goal is to give occasional presentations to civic clubs or groups of parents, you can accomplish that with a lower level of commitment than if your goal is to develop speaking as a source of income or to create a series of workshops that you present on a regular basis.

❏ IMPROVING AND GROWING AS A SPEAKER

If you discovered several areas for strengthening in order to do the kinds of presentations or workshops you hope to give, do not despair. You can become a better, more confident, and more experienced speaker. Remember Demosthenes, the great Greek orator who suffered from a speech impediment that he cured by putting stones in his mouth while he practiced his speeches. Legend has it that he then developed his powerful delivery by practicing speaking along the sea so he could be heard over the ocean's roar. With effective methods and persistent practice, you can overcome any weakness you now have as a speaker. You can speed up your improvement process by using some of the methods in the rest of this chapter.

Watch and Listen to Other Speakers

Listen to others' speeches and pay attention to what makes their presentations engaging as well as what distracts from their effectiveness. Look for techniques you want to incorporate into your own speaking toolkit. Watch and listen to anchors and reporters on television newscasts and news magazine programs. Notice what makes them compelling. Keep in mind that they are usually working from a teleprompter script, so they appear and sound more polished than you can expect of yourself when speaking live to a group. But you can learn from the way they use their voices, inflection, pauses, and emphasis. Watch political speeches to see what to do and what to avoid. One lesson I almost always take away from most political speeches is how hard it is to read a speech well, and why it is better to avoid reading it altogether if at all possible. Learn by watching other speakers, but remember that you will have your own unique style.

Start Collecting Content and Ideas

Gather resources you can use to make speech preparation easier. Keep a file or notebook for topics, openings, stories, statistics, examples, and quotes to use in future speeches. If you have one or two topics that you want to speak about, clip articles and cartoons related to the topic. Imagine a possible audience and sketch an outline for a presentation on your chosen topic. Decide on the three main points you would make. Then watch for examples and illustrations as you go through your day. Keep notepads handy in your car, by your bed, and in your office so you can write down ideas or examples when you think of them.

Practice Regularly

Speak regularly to keep in practice. As with any skill, you will become rusty if you do not practice. If you do not have any speaking engagements during a given week, practice giving your presentation to an empty room. Each time you practice, focus on improving or enhancing a particular aspect of your speaking. One time you may focus on increasing your energy or vocal variety. Another time you may work on adding drama to your stories and examples. Increase your mastery and ease each time, and you will be surprised at how quickly your speaking improves.

Record Your Speeches

Record your speeches to learn how you can improve. Audiotaping is good. Videotaping is even better, because you not only hear but see your nonverbal as well as your verbal patterns. Is it enjoyable to watch yourself give a speech? Not usually. You are learning a skill and will probably be critical of much that you see on the tape. The way to learn the most is to watch it more than once so you get past the initial reaction of hearing and seeing yourself recorded. Then you can start identifying the specific areas you want to improve. Ask yourself as you watch or listen: "What could I do differently that would most improve my presentation?" Perhaps you discovered that you use too many vocal pauses—*uh's* or *you know's* or other repetitive filler words. Practice changing that one aspect of your presentation content and style until you are able to speak without filling the pauses with them. Give and record the presentation again. Watch the tape to see how you have been able to improve and what more you can do with this aspect. Notice what about the changes worked best and how they improved the speech. Once you have mastered those changes, decide what would be the next biggest improvement you can make. Keep repeating the process, one specific improvement at a time.

Form a Peer Coaching Group

Form a presentation-skills peer coaching group with other coaches or therapists who are also interested in enhancing their speaking. Set regular meetings at which you discuss speaking ideas and topics and, most important, take turns presenting and getting feedback on what works and what could be better. Make sure you agree to guidelines for structuring the meetings and giving feedback. The emphasis should be on what works well and how something could be improved rather than on pointing out faults and mistakes.

Take a Class or Workshop

Take a class or workshop in public speaking or presentation skills. Classes are often offered at a reasonable cost through a local community college or adult education program. Workshops are also available in many communities as 1- or 2-day intensives. Dale Carnegie Training offers classes and workshops in many communities. As an alternative, consider taking an acting or improvisational theater class. While you will not learn how to prepare a presentation in an acting class, you will gain experience and learn techniques that can make you a better speaker.

The National Speakers Association (NSA) offers workshops that are geared toward professional speakers and those who want to be. Professional membership in NSA requires substantial professional speaking experience. The current requirement for membership is at least 20 paid speaking engagements in the previous year or $25,000 in annual speaking fees. Through the Academy for Professional Speaking, they offer programs for people wanting to learn how to speak professionally. Many state chapters of NSA also offer speaker's schools and other workshops for those who want to become better speakers. See the Resources section for more details.

Join Toastmasters

Join a local chapter of Toastmasters International. Toastmasters is a self-help organization with chapters in most parts of the country. Groups meet every week or two, and participants prepare speeches and speak to the group frequently. The group gives feedback and support. The purpose is to help people become more confident and effective speakers in their work or business. For more information about the nearest chapter, see Toastmasters in the Resources section.

Attend a Speaking Circle Event

Participate in one of Speaking Circles International's programs. Speaking Circles are weekly and biweekly speaking workshops, mostly on the West Coast, in which participants learn to be themselves in front of the group. Developed by Lee Glickstein, who started the program to help himself overcome his own severe stage fright, the groups teach specific processes for connecting with an audience. Leaders and participants give positive feedback. They have an excellent home study-guide available through their Web site. For more information, see Speaking Circles International in the Resources section.

Get a Speaking Coach

Work with a speaking or presentations coach. Some speaking coaches work primarily with helping clients overcome their fears and become more effective speakers. Others focus on helping their clients become professional speakers. Still others can help with both. You can go to coachvillereferral.com, coachu.com, and coachfederation.org to search their listings for coaches specializing in speaking or presentations. You can also do a Google or Yahoo! search for *speaking coach* or *presentations coach* to find coaches with this specialty.

Get Started

As you learn more about the process of preparing and giving presentations, you will be able to decide what will help you become a better speaker. So now, let's dive in and start deciding about possible topics for your presentations.

CHAPTER 3

Deciding What
to Talk About

CHOOSING A TOPIC IS a lot like choosing the destination for a trip. All other decisions rest on knowing where you are going. Making a good and clear decision about where you are going will have a major impact on how enjoyable and successful the trip is.

We will talk first about choosing the *topic* for your presentation. The topic is what the presentation is about—the subject. Later in this chapter we will discuss how to create an interesting and intriguing *title*—the one-sentence name that will appear in a program or that the program chairperson will announce.

❏ CHOOSING A TOPIC

One approach is to give presentations on topics that you are asked to speak about. A therapist might be asked: "Could you give a presentation to our organization about stress management?" or "Would you talk to our teachers about helping children cope with their fears about violence." A coach might be invited to speak on effective goal-setting, balancing priorities, or developing emotional intelligence.

One difficulty with choosing your topics based on invitations you receive is that organizations may have only a vague idea of what the presentation should be about. You may spend considerable time helping them clarify the topic and understand their needs, only to realize that you do not want to give a presentation on that topic or with that slant.

If you choose your topics according to what organizations ask for, you may never be asked to give the same presentation twice. You probably do not have the time to develop a new presentation on a different topic each time you speak. Furthermore, you will not be able to keep developing and improving a presentation unless you can give the speech more than once.

Most speakers choose topics that they want to talk about, and then find ways to adapt those presentations to meet the needs of specific audiences. To connect with your audience, you will have to adapt your topic to fit them. This can usually be done without abandoning your preferred topic.

❑ WHAT MAKES A GOOD TOPIC FOR A PRESENTATION?

A good topic for almost any presentation is one (a) that deals with a problem or need (b) that you are interested in, (c) that you know well or are willing to learn about in depth, (d) that can be used with or easily adapted for a number of audiences, (e) that your prospective clients (or professional colleagues) will want to know more about, (f) that your services relate to or help solve, and (g) that is specific enough to address in the time allotted for the presentation. Let's look more closely at these characteristics of a good topic.

A good topic *deals with a problem or need*. Almost any subject can be turned into an interesting presentation. But if you address a *problem* or *need* related to the topic, you will make the topic more engaging to the audience. Let's say you decide to talk about the importance of listening. You could make it more engaging by focusing on why it is so hard to listen. If you want to talk about goal setting, you could make it more engaging by focusing on the biggest mistakes most people make in setting goals. A story or novel is not engaging unless the main character is caught up in a conflict. In a similar way, presentations do not grab us unless they speak to problems or needs we would like to solve. The most positive, inspirational speech starts with a problem. The inspiration comes from the stories of how someone overcomes or deals with the problem.

To say it another way, a good topic should have an element of tension. The tension is almost always about a conflict between what is and what could be. For example, "Differences between women and men" implies some tension, but it would not be as engaging as "What men and women could learn from each other." The latter implies that there is a problem with the way things are, that things could be different, and that you are offering a possible solution.

Another advantage of focusing your topic on a problem is that it provides a ready-made direction for your presentation. First you explore the problem (its scope, its causes, its effects); then you present and describe possible solutions or alternatives. This is not the only way to structure a presentation, but it is one of the simplest and most effective. We will talk more about this in Chapter 5, "Planning and Preparing Your Presentation."

A good topic is *something that you are interested in.* One reason this is important is because a good topic is one you can use over and over again with different audiences. This allows you to shorten your preparation time and increase your comfort and familiarity with the topic. If you are not that interested, you will quickly become bored and boring. You may put only perfunctory time and effort into preparing the speech or workshop. You will probably cover the topic in a routine or superficial way. And you will not be able to put *yourself* into the presentation—your passion, enthusiasm, and caring.

A good topic is *one that you know well or are willing to learn about in depth.* The advantage of choosing a topic that you already know well is that you will need less time to research and prepare, and you will be able to draw on experiences and stories you have. For example, many therapists and coaches already have more than enough knowledge about stress, including knowledge from their own experience, to give a presentation. In less than 30 minutes, without referring to any books or files, they could outline a simple, informal presentation on "three strategies to take better care of yourself starting now." If I were asked to give that presentation 10 minutes from now, I would probably focus on listening to what our bodies are telling us, learning to identify the sources of our stress, and taking responsibility for meeting our needs. I could as easily choose to talk about learning to breathe, learning to let go of tension, and learning to confront what we have been resisting or avoiding. My point is that most therapists and coaches know a lot about most of these topics. In terms of content, we could talk about one to three of them easily, teaching basic techniques in the moment, telling a few stories about them, and suggesting some ways to continue applying them.

EXERCISE 3.1. What You Know About

As a way of demonstrating that you already have within you topics for a few different talks, take 10 minutes now and jot down three topic areas that you are interested in and knowledgeable about. Brainstorm three to five main points you could make about one of the topics.

You probably know enough about five or six topics, or more, to give an informal presentation with less than an hour to prepare a simple outline.

A good topic is *one that can be used with or easily adapted for a number of audiences.* You will not be able to create totally new presentations each time you speak, as we have said. You need a topic that will work with many of the audiences that you will want to give presentations to. We will talk about finding and choosing audiences in Chapter 4, but in choosing a topic you should consider whether it is so specialized that you will have difficulty finding audiences that will want to hear about it. If your specialty as a therapist is working with families of people with chronic degenerative diseases, you could choose a topic such as dealing with the stress of chronic degenerative disease and then adapt the topic and the title for addressing specific audiences, such as families of people with multiple sclerosis, rheumatoid arthritis, or Lou Gehrig's disease. This is a fairly specific niche, and if you wanted to use your expertise and experience to broaden your niche, you might decide on a topic such as coping with chronic illness in the family. This broader topic could be slanted to work with many community-based and health-related groups, especially if you talked about loss of functioning from chronic illness as a continuum that all families experience at some time.

Coaches who specialize in working with parents might want to choose a topic such as "It takes a village to raise a child" if they want to be able to give the presentation to groups that included others besides parents. If, instead, they chose a topic such as how to improve one's parenting skills overnight, they would limit themselves to audiences consisting mostly or entirely of parents.

You may develop a presentation that focuses on stress on the job and then slant it a bit differently depending on your audience. If you developed a basic presentation on overlooked sources of stress and what to do about them, you might have six sources of stress that you *could* talk about: environmental noise, inadequate planning, catastrophizing, sleep deprivation, difficulty setting boundaries, and putting off making small decisions. (Of course, there are many others you might choose for your list.) In a given presentation, you would only use one to three of them. Your choice would depend on the audience and the slant of your topic. To a group of executives, you might choose to speak on sleep deprivation, catastrophizing, and putting off making small decisions as overlooked sources of stress. To a group of middle managers, you might choose inadequate planning, catastrophizing, and difficulty setting boundaries. To a group of parents, you might want to talk about sleep deprivation, difficulty setting boundaries, and putting off making small decisions. If you were speaking to a group of small-business owners, you could choose *any* of them because they could identify with all of them.

If one of your specialties as a therapist is sleep disorders, you might focus your whole presentation on the effects of sleep deprivation and how to get more sleep. But if you are a performance enhancement coach, *one* of your points might be about sleep deprivation as an important factor affecting performance and you might give some tips on improving sleep. But you might also talk about the effect on performance from inadequate planning and putting off making small decisions.

Here is a slightly different approach. Let's say you are a life coach and you want to talk about the value of balance in one's life. You may encourage your audiences to look at how balanced their lives are in certain key areas: work, personal, family, spiritual, and financial. You might have a series of questions you ask every audience, and you might use them with every audience. But your examples and suggestions would be different for a group of young parents than for an audience of business owners.

Therapists and coaches may take different approaches in focusing or slanting their topics. For example, one psychotherapist who wanted to attract more female managers and executives into her practice came up with a topic: "Seven Habits of Success for Women in Business." This might be a good topic for a business-oriented speech by a coach, but it was less likely to attract psychotherapy clients. The therapist changed her topic to "Dealing With the Special Stresses of Being a Woman in Business." This way she could address women's "pain," demonstrate her understanding of their situation, and offer hope and encouragement.

A good topic is *one that your prospective clients (or professional colleagues) will want to know more about and that your services relate to or help solve.* The easiest way to find a topic that will interest your prospective clients (or professional colleagues) is to focus the topic on a problem or challenge that your clients or colleagues face. If one of your client specialties is working with dual career couples, you could speak about stress on the job, but a better topic might be stresses of dual-career relationships.

If you are coach or therapist with no real interest or expertise in attention deficit disorder (ADD), it would not make sense to agree to speak on ADD simply because that is the topic the organization wants to hear about. But if you are a therapist or coach with ADD as a specialty, it would be an ideal topic for you. If you are asked to speak on a topic that is not a good fit for you, instead of saying no, suggest an alternative topic that would work for you.

There is nothing wrong with giving a presentation on a hobby or interest that is unrelated to your practice specialties. You may enjoy the change of focus and meet some interesting people. Your audience may respond well to hearing a professional talk about something that has nothing to do with work. If, for example, you are a psychologist who collects rare stamps, you *may* get some new clients from a talk on stamp collecting, but you are likely to get more clients from a talk on "the importance of exercising the mind as well as the body" or "how our hobbies help keep us healthy." Coaches who grow orchids may get some clients from presentations on orchid culture, but they may get even more from a speech on how to cultivate one's passion for success or how to get more done by "wasting" time.

A good topic is *one that is specific enough to address in the time allotted for the presentation.* Choosing the topic for your presentation means choosing the subject you will talk about. It also means deciding what aspects of the subject you will address and what you will omit from the discussion. Choosing a specific aspect of a topic makes it easier to prepare the presentation. Suppose you decide you want to do a presentation on communication. Communication is so broad and general that you probably would not know where to start. You might fall into the trap of spending the first half of your presentation defining terms and making general points about communication. This is a common pitfall of professional presentations and a common reason why they are often boring.

If you decide in advance what aspect of your subject you will talk about, you can go straight to the meat of your presentation without a long preamble. The key is to make the topic specific enough for the time you have. One aspect of communication would be communication in the workplace, but this is still too broad unless you are preparing a weeklong workshop. Listening skills for the workplace is more specific, but unless you deal with many aspects of that topic, it is still too broad. Listening as a time-saving technique or three communication skills men and women can learn from one another may be getting specific enough for a presentation to a business or community-oriented audience.

How do you decide whether a topic is specific enough? You will learn from experience about what works, but here are some guidelines that can help:

1. For presentations or speeches other than workshops, you should be able to state your core message in one sentence. The core message is your main point. It is what you want your audience to take away from your presentation. If you cannot state the core message in one sentence, either your topic is too broad or you are not yet clear enough about what you want to say. For presentations or speeches of less than an hour, you should usually not have more than three main points, and never more than five main points. These are the points that make up your single core message. In the earlier example about overlooked sources of stress, the core message might be: You can significantly lower your moment-to-moment stress by doing something about three commonly overlooked sources of stress. The main points would be the three sources that you choose to talk about.

2. For a workshop or seminar of several hours, you need a topic that you can cover at a depth that fits your audience. A workshop for child psychologists, for example, would cover the topic of sleep problems of children at a different level than a workshop for parents. The topic should be focused enough that you do not rush or overwhelm them, but also so that you do not bore them because you are going too slowly. For most speeches and workshops, less is more. One of the most common speaking mistakes is to try to cram in too much information.

3. You can increase interest in your topic by choosing a subject that is in the news or is related to a current trend. After the 9/11 terrorist attacks, many organizations wanted presentations on coping with trauma and dealing with fear and anxiety.

Emotional intelligence was a hot topic for several years after Daniel Goleman's bestselling book introduced the term. If you tie your topic to a trend or news event, you risk its becoming outdated after media interest dies down. But if you choose a topic with an interest that will continue after the immediate news stories fade, you are not relying on the news story for the main appeal. An example is the Columbine shootings. If, as a therapist, you choose to speak on some aspect of violence in schools, the interest in that topic will not go away just because Columbine becomes a more distant memory.

❏ WHERE DO YOU START IF YOU DON'T HAVE A TOPIC?

One good place to start is to look for ideas as close as your own bookshelves or go to a nearby large library or bookstore and spend a few hours looking at book titles and Tables of Contents in the psychology, self-help, relationship, career, and business sections. The advantage of a bookstore is that everything will be up-to-date and the most popular books will not be checked out. Take along note cards and pen to jot down topics and titles that get your attention and, most important, that get your creative juices flowing. Note the topics where you find yourself thinking, "I would like to do a presentation on that" or "I could do a workshop about that," or "That's exactly what my clients are dealing with or want to know about."

Notice *what kinds of topics* you are drawn to. Are they about relationships or individual self-improvement? Are they are about dealing with difficult moods such as anxiety and depression, or are they about personal development such as creativity and empowerment? Are they about concerns in one's personal life or about issues related to work and employment?

Some of the topics you will be drawn to may be subjects you want to learn more about for yourself. Do not rule out a topic merely because you need or want to learn more about it. A good topic is *one you already know well or are willing to learn about in depth.* Sometimes your best topic is the one you most want to learn more about. You will be willing to invest the time and energy into learning about it, and you may also be in tune with what others want to know.

An alternative to going to a large bookstore is to use the Internet. The listings at www.amazon.com, the online bookstore, can be searched or browsed by subject and key words. For most topics, there are lists of best books or favorite books that others have compiled. A helpful feature is that you can view and print the Tables of Contents of many books. If you decide you want to do a presentation on developing and using intuition at work, you could search for book titles on that topic and look at the Tables of Contents of many of them, all from your own computer. I am not advocating plagiarizing or stealing ideas. I am encouraging you to use others' ideas to trigger and stimulate your own thinking and creativity.

Another approach to finding presentation topics using the Internet is to go to "portal" Web sites such as aol.com, msn.com, and ivillage.com. These sites allow you to choose general subject areas such as health, relationships, and work, and then choose from more and more specific listings of topics in these general subject areas. For more specific topics, you can view magazine articles, recent news, columns, links, bulletin boards, and even topic-oriented chat areas.

Internet searches can be time-consuming and lead you down numerous dead-end and distracting paths. You may want to set a time limit on your surfing for a topic to keep from wasting time that could be better spent on self-reflection or browsing at the bookstore or library.

Another good method for coming up with presentation topics is to use the Topic Idea Worksheet that follows. To brainstorm about possible topics for your presentations, you answer a series of questions. The Topic Idea Worksheets in this chapter contain examples of answers to show you how the process can work. You may want to jot down the questions on a pad or in a word processing document, so you can add ideas as they occur.

WORKSHEET 3.1. Topic Ideas for Community Presentations

1. *What are your clients' challenges, frustrations, and problems? What concerns do your clients ask or talk about most often, including concerns related to their work, family, relationships, health, emotions, and age? If you are moving into a new client niche or specialty, include their challenges, frustrations, and problems to the degree that you know them.*

I recommend that you think of each current and recent client, one at a time, and write down the challenges, frustrations, problems, questions, and concerns that each one talked about. You will think of many more examples using this method than if you think of your clients as a group. You might answer these questions for yourself and your friends, also, since your challenges and frustrations are probably the same ones faced by many of your clients or prospective clients.

Therapist example: Feeling depressed; having money problems or being worried about money; feeling stressed; being unhappy with marriage; having communication problems or conflict with partner; worrying about school or emotional problems for children; having conflict with teenage children; experiencing empty-nest issues; being overwhelmed by parenting demands; having conflict with parents; dealing with aging parents; feeling stuck in an abusive relationship; dealing with substance abuse; feeling overwhelmed by or unhappy with work; experiencing conflict at work; being worried about job layoffs; trying to find a job; wanting to change careers; going through a separation or divorce; grieving the loss of a parent, spouse, or sibling; dealing with chronic illness or pain; dealing with shame and guilt; having difficulty meeting people or making friends; experiencing difficulty with anger in oneself or others; being too much of a people pleaser; being a perfectionist; feeling self-critical; having spiritual questions; experiencing sexual problems (lack of interest, mismatch with partner, performance issues, problems with pornography); having sleep problems; wasting time watching TV or Internet surfing; experiencing posttraumatic stress from terrorist attacks, robbery, or rape; having difficulty saying no or setting boundaries; feeling social anxiety or phobia; having stage fright; experiencing eating disorders.

Coach example: feeling overwhelmed with workload; trying to balance personal and family life with work; dealing with irritating colleague; wanting to make good decisions; not being a good listener; not being good at marketing and selling; difficulty deciding on priorities; not being good at planning (would rather shoot from the hip); not being good at following through with details; having difficulty with delegating; feeling guilty about taking time off; not being good at running meetings; not being promoted as quickly as expected; not working well in teams; leading teams; having worries about layoffs; feeling guilty about having to lay people off; not having enough time to think; having to travel too much; working from a cubicle; not liking telephone meetings; not having support staff; feeling unclear about expectations. Possible topics generated from the responses above:

For therapists: Improving communication; improving relationships; creating time and space to follow one's dreams and passions; dealing with transitions at different life stages; dealing with workplace stress.

For coaches: Starting your own business; finding the time to do more of what you want; making time for relationships; creating balance; understanding the importance of appreciation; setting your own priorities; communicating effectively; learning how to be creative in what you do.

2. *What changes and transitions are occurring in your clients' (and prospective clients') lives and world? In yours?*

Therapist example: Growing older; having children (and grandchildren) who are growing up; having grandchildren; graduating and starting to work; getting married; getting divorced; meeting new people; losing a job; changing a job or career; starting a business; retiring; moving to a new house or community; getting a job promotion with increased responsibilities; experiencing the death of parents, spouse, siblings, or peers; having health problems; feeling anxious about terrorism.

Coach example: Technology is changing everything; 24/7 and global marketplace; layoffs; change that is so fast that it is difficult/impossible to plan; new boss; new office; new competition; new accountability practices; new procedures; teams keep changing.

Possible topics generated from the responses above:

For therapists: The emotional aspects of growing older; the relationship aspects of growing older; how change (or stress) affects relationships; dealing with reality when things go wrong; the changing face of work; dealing with our limitations; the basis of our security.

For coaches: Managing or dealing with constant change; new workplace ethics; strategies for dealing with uncertainty; planning in the face of change; how to get off to a quick (and good) start in new situations; teamwork is not just for the workplace.

3. *What do your clients (and prospective clients) want from life or in their lives? What are their dreams, and yours?*

    Therapist example: To be happy; to have peace of mind; to experience less stress; to have happy and healthy children; to enjoy a romantic/sexual relationship; to have good relationships with partner/spouse, children, parents, peers; to have satisfying and productive work; to feel competent; to feel confident; to feel good about themselves; to have financial security; to feel they are making a difference; to have time to enjoy life; to be enthusiastic about life; to create and be creative; to express themselves; to feel they can be themselves; to have their own business; to travel; to lose weight or feel good about their bodies; to be healthy; to be pain free; to achieve a particular dream (write a book, climb a mountain, fly a plane, go to Paris, etc.).

Coach example: To work for oneself; to make more money; to have time to spend with family; to have time to enjoy money; to have time to think; to have more friends; to do more socializing; to have more free time; to get more exercise; to get more sleep; to be happy; to travel less on business; to feel competent; to be recognized and appreciated at work; to create and be creative; to be healthy; to achieve a particular dream (write a book, climb a mountain, fly a plane, go to Paris, etc.).

Possible topics generated from the responses above:

For therapists: The emotional aspects of money; the importance of purpose; finding what makes us happy; the elements of a healthy relationship; our changing relationships with family and friends; the role of creativity in well-being; letting yourself be seen and heard; exploring your dreams; what gives life meaning?

For coaches: Finding and making time for what matters; how to be a friend; discovering and getting what you want; how you can feel better about yourself; so you're thinking about starting a business; what we know about staying healthy.

4. *Which of the topic areas above relate to the services you provide or plan to offer?*

5. *Which of the topic areas that interest you are you knowledgeable about or willing to learn about?*

Therapist example: Willing to learn about any of them, but know the most about improving communication, improving relationships, and dealing with transitions. Know about stress generally, but not so much about workplace stress.

Coach example: Willing to learn about most of them, but know the least about starting a business, except my own. Know a lot about communicating effectively and developing relationships. Also know a lot about life balance and creativity on and off the job.

7. *Which of these areas would be most helpful and interesting to your prospective clients? If you are moving into a new client niche or specialty, include those prospective clients in your thinking.*

Therapist example: Improving communication and dealing with transitions, for sure. Improving relationships would probably be interesting, but what comes to mind is improving relationships with oneself as well as others. Creating time and space to follow one's dreams and passions is also an issue that many clients struggle with in various ways.

Coach example: Having balance in life; creating time for what's important; communicating effectively; having ability to do creative problem solving.

8.   *Imagine you are presenting a talk on some of the topics you have identified above. Now think of a client or clients for whom this talk would be particularly interesting. What questions might these clients ask about the topic?*

Therapist example: How can I improve my relationship with my spouse? How can I deal with my anger more effectively? How can I create more time for me? How do I deal with the death of my spouse (my children leaving home, my chronic illness, losing my job)? Is how I feel normal?

Coach example: How can I start my own business and make it work financially? How can I find more time for what's important to me? How can I balance the demands of work and family? How can I enjoy more of what I do? How can I be a more effective leader? How can I have a more fulfilling relationship with my spouse?

8.   *Think of several of your clients, one at a time, and think about what they would need to know about the topic areas you have identified to make their lives better in these areas. Write down your ideas as they come to mind.*

Therapist example: How to communicate clearly without provoking; how to set limits and boundaries with others; how to take time for oneself without feeling guilty; how to deal with the inner critic; how to create a process for understanding and dealing with change and transition; how to nurture a relationship (with partner, with friends, with children); how to stop procrastinating; how to handle anxiety.

Coach example: How to set and follow priorities; how to set limits and boundaries; how to be more aware of inner process and self talk; how to listen and communicate more effectively; how to relax and manage stress; how to make the transition to being self-employed.

9. *Choose the topics that appeal to you from the ideas you have generated so far. Express each one in a phrase, sentence, or question. Refine and revise them until you have come up with one or more presentation topic that you like.*

   Therapist example: The Power of Yes and No (setting boundaries, making decisions, communicating clearly); Letting Go Without Giving Up (grieving losses, understanding change and transition); Listening to Your Life (self care, taking time for oneself, paying attention to inner process); The Meaning of Our Emotions (handling strong emotions); What Relationships Need to Grow (nurturing relationships).

   Coach example: Listening As a Way of Leading; How to Get What You Need and Do More of What You Want; The Importance of Seemingly Unimportant Decisions; Learning to Work with Flow.

WORKSHEET 3.2. Topic Ideas for Professional Colleague
Presentations

1. *What are your colleagues' challenges, frustrations, and problems?
   What concerns do your colleagues talk about most often? What do
   your colleagues want to know more about?*

   Therapist example: Managed care; paperwork; short-term
   therapy; new treatment modalities; marketing one's practice;
   couples' issues; attention deficit disorder (ADD); dialectical
   behavior therapy; substance abuse issues in treatment.

   Coach example: Attracting more clients; developing a niche;
   mastering client retention; establishing self-care for coaches;
   marketing to businesses and corporations; making the transition from therapy to coaching; handling the details and paperwork; getting in touch with spirituality; understanding the
   current economy.

2. *What changes and transitions are occurring in your and your colleagues' professional world? What are the new developments in your
   field?*

   Therapist example: Managed care and insurance changes;
   HIPAA regulations; electronic filing; new medications.

   Coach example: Field itself is new and changing; new people
   entering the field; higher standards and expectations for
   coaches; coaching being recognized by media and business.

3. *What areas do you specialize in? What knowledge, experience,
   training, or expertise do you have that other colleagues might find
   helpful or want to know more about?*

   Therapist example: attention deficit disorder (ADD) in
   adults; dialectical behavior therapy (DBT); substance abuse
   treatment issues.

   Coach example: business coaching; corporate experience;
   sales and marketing background; understanding of executive
   role and pressures.

4.   *Which of these would you be interested in developing into a presentation or workshop?*

   Therapist example: How to Talk About Alcohol Abuse With Your Patients; Diagnosing and Treating Attention Deficit Disorder (ADD) in Adults.

   Coach example: What Every Coach Needs to Know About Business; Understanding Your Executive Clients; Marketing for Coaches.

❏ GETTING FEEDBACK ON YOUR TOPICS

When you have tentatively chosen one or more possible topics, ask at least three people whether the topic sounds interesting to them. Explain to them that you are developing a speech for business, community, or professional groups, and you want to choose a topic that will interest people like them. Ask them what about the topic interests them and what they think of when they hear the topic. Ask them what problems they see with any of your topics. If you have started thinking of titles, ask for their reaction and suggestions to these as well. Seek out people who would be representative of those for whom the topic is designed. If the topic is for professional colleagues, ask your colleagues. If the presentation would be for a more general audience, ask people who would be typical of that audience.

Even though your primary goal is getting feedback on the topic, if you ask them what interests them about the topic, you may also get some ideas for the content as well.

Take notes or write down their ideas as soon as you leave. If you have not already started a file, this is the time to start keeping one for each presentation you are planning.

❏ CREATING A GREAT TITLE

Until now we have been talking primarily about topics—what the presentation would be about. Now let's talk about titles.

Why are titles important? Titles are like headlines in the newspaper. They are designed to give some idea of what the story is about and to entice you to read it.

Creating a title is difficult for many people. The title needs to be clever, but not too cute; enticing but not overstated. The title has to be specific enough to be interesting, but not too restrictive if you need to change your emphasis to fit your audience.

One way to start is with a description of what your speech is about. Until you come up with something better, you can always use that description as your title. For example: "What Men and Women Don't

Understand About Each Other" is a good title as well as a basic description of the topic. For presentations to professional colleagues and workshop titles, a straightforward description is often the most appropriate title. For community groups, however, you can increase interest with a more interesting title.

Some examples of "quick and easy" titles can take the form of:

- "The ABC's of . . ."
- "Myths of . . ."
- "Secrets of . . ."
- "_____101" (as in Listening 101 or Parenting 101)
- "The Keys to . . ."
- "Three Lessons about . . ."
- "New Ways to . . ."
- "How to . . ."
- "The Most Important . . ."
- "What You Need to Know About . . ."
- "The Biggest Mistakes People Make About _____(and How to Avoid Them)"

Even though these may not be exciting titles, they give you flexibility to take the speech in a variety of directions.

We talked earlier about browsing at books to trigger ideas for topics. Another good place to find ideas for titles is in magazines. As you have probably noticed, including numbers in titles is popular in books and magazine titles. One reason is that lists do not require careful transitions between points because people don't expect them to be closely connected.

Pick a title that you are comfortable with and avoid hype. You want people to trust you, so your title should encourage trust. For example, "Say Good-bye to Stress Forever" and "How to Stop Your Children from Fighting Every Time" are not believable titles. It is better to have people feel they got more than they expected than to feel you did not deliver what your title promised.

For example, you might choose a title to match the way you organized your content. A presentation on listening that gives a sequence of steps might be titled "The ABCs of Listening." A similar presentation organized around misconceptions about listening might be called "The Myths of Listening." A presentation to professional colleagues on listening might be called "The Dynamics of Empathic Listening." A similar presentation given as an in-service for nurses might be called "How to Listen to Patients Even When You Don't Have Time," but retitled for parents as "How to Listen to Your Children When You Don't Have Time and Don't Feel Like It Anyway" or "How to Listen to Your Teen Even If They Aren't Talking." A presentation for business people could be called "How to Make a Great First Impression—Listen!" or for salespeople could be "Want to Sell More? Shut Up and Listen!"

You can also increase interest in your topic by taking a position or expressing a point of view in the title. Instead of using the title "The Keys to Life Balance," you might take a position with the title "You *Can* Have More Balance in Your Life." Why is a title with a point of view more interesting? In part, it lets you put more of yourself into it. It also gives the audience something to react to or "push against." It is harder for them to stay neutral or unengaged in their reactions. Of course, taking a position or expressing a point of view will not be appropriate for all types of presentations. Scientific, research-based presentations may take a point of view, but a subtle one.

As with topics, ask several people what they think of your title before you use it. They may hear a meaning that you did not intend. If you are speaking to an international audience, make sure you are not using a phrase that would be misunderstood or offensive to people from another country or culture.

Whatever title you choose, do not let your title lock you in. You may submit your title in advance and then find that the title no longer fits the speech you want to give. It is better to throw out the title than to try to make your speech fit it. You can always begin your speech by saying that you have changed your focus since submitting the title for the program.

As long as you explain your shift in focus, most people in the audience will not give it a second thought.

❏ POSSIBLE TOPICS FOR THERAPISTS AND COACHES

Here are some examples of speech topics and titles that could be used by both coaches and therapists, perhaps with different slants. Not all of them would be appropriate for all audiences or speakers, but the list is intended to be an idea generator. A list of additional topics for therapists is at the end of this section.

- Stress
- Relationships
- Communication
- Change and Transition
- Understanding People, Including Ourselves
- Parenting
- How to Get a Good Night's Sleep
- Dealing with Difficult People
- Does Someone You Know Have ADHD?
- Constructive Ways to Deal with Our Fears
- Understanding Our Dreams
- How "Just Talking" Can Change Our Lives
- Dealing with Life's Setbacks
- The Emotional Meaning of Money
- What to Expect Emotionally When You're Expecting
- Is There Hope for Families?
- Living in Step Families
- How to Be a Friend
- Understanding Our Emotions
- Dealing with Emotions on the Job (Yours *and* Theirs)
- Why It's Good to Be Different: Understanding Personality Type
- How to Make Good Decisions
- You Can Learn to Put Off Procrastinating
- How to Relax

- How to Develop Your Intuition
- How to Encourage Another Person
- How to Deal with a Difficult Boss
- Do We Have to Do It All?: Reflections from a Recovering Perfectionist
- What Makes You Sing?: Rediscovering Joy in Everyday Life
- Keeping Your Mind Young or How to Exercise Your Mind as Well as Your Body
- We Can Start Feeling Better About Our Bodies
- Teaching Our Children Values
- Learning to Deal Constructively with Anger
- Time Management Isn't Just for Business
- The Miracle of Memory
- How to Develop a Better Memory
- What Is Healthy Religion?
- When Religion Becomes Destructive
- The Power of Visualization
- Learning to Let Go
- Why Families Are So Important
- How People Change
- What's Wrong with Needing People?
- How What We Eat Affects Our Moods
- Understanding the Patterns of Adult Development
- Is There Such a Thing as a Midlife Crisis and Am I Having One?
- Making Sense of Our Moods
- Learning to Deal with Change
- Grieving Life's Losses
- Finding Your Way Through Separation and Divorce
- How to Help Another Person
- Creativity as a Window of Our Soul
- The Role of Creativity in Success
- Problem-Solving for Healthy Living
- The Things That Make Us Human
- The Hidden Power of Shame

- What Our Feelings Can Tell Us
- The Need for Wisdom in Our Information Society
- How to Change a Habit
- Are You Out of Your Mind or Just Out of Touch with Your Body?
- Getting Off to a Good Start in a Relationship
- Why Smart People Do Dumb Things
- What Men and Women Can Learn from Each Other
- What You Can Do About Road Rage
- How to Stand Up for Yourself: Assertiveness for Shy People
- Learning to Negotiate for What You Need
- How Can We Be Good to Ourselves?
- You Can Learn to Say No
- Let's Talk About Sex
- What the Future Looks Like from Here
- Seven Ways to Start Working Smarter Today
- How to Use Your Whole Brain to Solve Problems
- How to Have More Energy
- The Power of Accepting Who You Are
- The Impact of Living With Integrity
- Everything You Always Wanted to Know About _____ (Goals, Managing Your Time, Getting Organized, Finding Balance, etc.)
- The Hidden Power of Caring
- What We All Need to Know About Diversity
- How To Plan
- How to Have Great Meetings
- Should You Start a Business?
- Talking with Our _____ (Children, Teens, Spouses, etc.)
- What Happens When the Child Becomes the Parent: Dealing with Aging Parents
- What Makes People Happy?
- Should We Always Forgive?
- Emotional Intelligence at Work: The Keys to True Success
- Emotional Intelligence: How to Educate the Whole Child

- How to Really Help Your Child with _____ (School, Self-esteem, Relationships, etc.)
- How Relationships Help Keep Us Healthy
- Stress Is in Your Head But You Can Get It Out
- What We Know About What Motivates People

Psychotherapists often speak on clinical topics related to mental health and mental illness. Here are some additional examples of speech topics and titles to stimulate thinking for therapists.

- New Developments in Understanding or Treating Emotional Difficulties
- Emotional Issues in _____ (Chronic Illness, Aging, Divorce, etc.)
- Grief and Loss
- New Treatments for Postpartum Depression
- There's Help for Your Phobias
- What Is Biofeedback and Can It Help You?
- What We *Can* Do About Violence in Our Communities
- It's Time to Talk About _____ (Rape, Spouse Abuse, Elder Abuse, Teen Suicide, Alcohol, etc.)
- What Everyone Needs to Know About Drugs (could be for parents, employers, etc.)
- What Works in Helping Alcoholics Recover?
- What You Need to Know About _____ (Sexual Harassment, Depression, Panic Attacks, Anxiety, Suicide, etc.)
- The Connection Between Spirituality and Mental Health
- Everything You Always Wanted to Know About Hypnosis

CHAPTER 4

Finding and Choosing Your Audiences

FINDING AUDIENCES FOR YOUR presentation can seem like a daunting task when you are starting out, but it is much easier than most people imagine. There are dozens of organizations in every community that would like to hear what you have to say. As you read this, a program chairperson in your community is wondering who she can find to give a program. One of your challenges is to find out about the groups that are looking for speakers and to make sure they find out about you.

Other audiences for your presentations do not hold regular meetings. They may be a department in a company, a staff of a nonprofit organization, a class at a local university, or an outreach event sponsored by a local hospital. If you follow the suggestions in this book for discovering speaking opportunities in your community, you will probably be surprised at the number of audiences who gather each day for presentations. In this chapter you will learn how to identify and line up presentations for existing audiences and groups. You will also learn how to create speaking opportunities, on your own or with others, and gather an audience for your presentation, workshop, or seminar.

❑ WHERE DO COACHES AND THERAPISTS SPEAK?

Therapists and coaches give presentations to audiences from the following types of groups.

Local Service and Community Organizations

Examples: The most familiar may be Kiwanis, Rotary, Lions, Optimists, and Civitan, but this category also includes religious organizations, self-help groups, men's and women's organizations, alumni organizations, ethnic support groups, neighborhood associations, garden clubs, singles groups, parent-teacher organizations, senior citizen organizations, special interest groups (Sierra Club, League of Women's Voters), sports groups, and study groups.

Types of presentations: Not all of these organizations have speeches at their regular meetings, but many of them do. Others may use speakers for special events or as part of a training or facilitated meeting for their members. The most common presentation is a 20-minute speech to a service club as part of their weekly or bimonthly meeting. These speeches are a way for club members to learn more about their community.

Advantages: Because many of these organizations have weekly meetings with speakers, and they do not pay their speakers, they are often the easiest speaking engagements to obtain and arrange. They are often eager to find more speakers. These organizations are usually lower threat audiences for new speakers. Because they have so many speakers, audiences do not expect a highly polished professional speech from everyone. They typically want to learn something they did not already know. They are there for their meeting, and an interesting presentation is a plus. Service organizations are also an excellent place to hone and improve your presentation skills. Many well-paid professional speakers say that they learned to speak well by giving lots of free speeches to service clubs. Another advantage is that service club audiences often include influential leaders from the community. In one presentation, you may be addressing the mayor or city manager, a bank president, a plant manager, and several business owners. The community leaders you meet through service club presentations can be influential in recommending you to others or in providing other speaking opportunities in the future.

Disadvantages: Since these organizations almost never pay speakers, you will be speaking for the experience and the exposure. You will not necessarily know in advance whether a particular service club is a good audience for your services. In the past, service clubs were mostly male, but that is changing with many of them. If you work mostly with women, for example, you might question whether this is worth your time and effort.

Local and Regional Business, Professional, and Trade Organizations

Examples: Among these are sales and marketing executives, chambers of commerce, networking organizations, Business and Professional Women, Associations of University Women, associations of realtors, the bar association (attorneys), medical societies, and dental associations.

Members of business and professional organizations join because they have a common business or professional interest. They may be in the same profession or they may share a concern for promoting business in general. Some people would classify certain service clubs, such as Rotary, as business and professional organizations because their members are also business and professional people.

Local and regional trade associations also fit into this category. A trade association is an organization of businesses of a certain category, such as the Association of Heating and Air Conditioning Contractors, the Home Builders Association, or the State Bankers Association. Often a regional or state trade association is affiliated with a national trade association.

Types of presentations: These organizations often meet monthly instead of weekly, and their presentations are more varied. The main characteristic of presentations for business and professional organizations is that they are more focused toward the specific group. While a presentation to a Kiwanis Club (service organization) might be on improving communication at home and at work, a presentation for a bar association group (lawyers) might be on listening skills for lawyers. These organizations will not be interested in a presentation unless it is pinpointed to their specific audience, and thus you must be able to target your talk to a variety of audiences.

Business, professional, and trade associations also sponsor special conferences and events that use speakers. A state trade association may hold a 2- or 3-day conference or convention with keynote speakers and breakout speakers. Keynote speakers address the entire conference and are usually intended as highlights of the gathering. Breakout sessions at conferences are short workshops offered on particular topics. They provide an opportunity for people to "break" into smaller groups according to their interests.

Chambers of commerce often organize business "expos" where their members set up booths or displays for their businesses. To attract more people, the organizers often schedule 1- to 2-hour seminars throughout the day on topics related to business. Coaches and therapists may give brief seminars on topics related to stress, work balance, or people skills.

Some trade associations sponsor training and continuing education events for their members. Although much of the training may be technical or trade-specific, trade associations may also be interested in offering a workshop on communication skills, stress management, or customer service, as long as it will be focused on their audience's specific needs.

Advantages: For coaches and therapists with a focus on business, professionals, or work/life issues, these organizations may provide audiences that match the coach's or therapist's interests and client profile. A few of these organizations may offer modest payment for a presentation. For conferences, training, and continuing education events sponsored by a trade association, the payment may be at the going professional speaking and training rates. Speaking at an association event can give exposure to many individuals and organizations that are members of the association. One presentation at an association event might open the door to several opportunities for speaking, training, or coaching within member organizations.

Disadvantages: Business and professional organizations focus on business-related issues. Therapists and coaches must be able to speak to the business issues in order to be asked to present. Business audiences often have a bias against so-called touchy-feely topics and presentations and may be turned off by discussions of what a therapist considers basic communication or feelings. Business and professional audiences generally have higher expectations of presentations than service and community organizations do. When an organization is paying the speaker more than a token amount, they may also expect a more polished presentation than when the speaker is donating time.

Local Businesses, Hospitals, Governmental Agencies, Schools, Libraries, Professional Practices, and Nonprofit Organizations

Examples: These include businesses of all sizes; hospitals; medical and other health care practices; retirement communities; stock brokerage firms; real estate firms; local police and fire departments; social service agencies; city and county governments; public and private schools including staff; local libraries; Red Cross, Habitat for Humanity, United Way agencies, and foundations.

Types of presentations: Presentations for these groups fall into two main types: (a) presentations for an organization's employees, volunteers, or board of directors, and (b) presentations sponsored by the organization for the public or for their clients.

Coaches and therapists may conduct training or mini-workshops ranging from 1 hour to 2 days long on topics such as stress management, customer service, communication skills (presentation skills, writing, listening, giving feedback), difficult people, time management, self-care, or critical incident debriefing (helping staff talk through their feelings after an upsetting event such as a robbery or attack at work). A business coach may be contracted to do presentations on strategic planning, financial management, marketing, management skills, team building, and other related topics.

Presentations for employees of businesses, government agencies, and health care facilities are often considered training and may be called lunch-and-learn seminars (because they are offered over lunch) or in-service training or workshops (because they are offered during the workday on topics directly related to the employees' work).

Hospitals and health care facilities may also use presentations for their staff on specific mental health issues such as recognizing depression or avoiding burnout. Therapists with a specific specialty may be able to do an in-service for a local Employee Assistance Program (EAP). Employee Assistance Programs provide crisis intervention and short-term counseling for employees of member organizations. Often EAPs are looking for specialists to keep them up to date and well informed. What this does for you is to let you meet their staff and their staff to meet you. Since EAPs usually make many referrals to community therapists, this can be an excellent opportunity to get on their list.

The other common type of presentation in this category is one sponsored by a business, hospital, or nonprofit organization. Hospitals may sponsor seminars and presentations for the community on health and wellness topics. Nonprofit organizations and libraries also sponsor presentations for the community, either as part of a series or as a special event. Businesses may sponsor an evening seminar for their clients or customers. A bank, stock brokerage, or accounting or law firm, for example, may sponsor a seminar for customers on managing money or for business customers on making better business decisions. A coach or therapist could be one of the speakers and might focus on the emotional and relationship aspects of how to be more comfortable talking about money. (Suze Orman has made this a popular topic with her books and presentations on the laws of money.)

A variation of the cosponsored seminar that may interest business coaches is one directed toward business executives. These seminars, often called executive briefings, usually last between 60 and 90 minutes and are designed to give executives up-to-the-minute information about an important business topic such as how to keep top performers, new changes in human resource legislation, technology advances that are changing business, key economic trends, and so on. A business coach could team up with a business lawyer to talk about changes in human resource regulations and their implications. Executive briefings are usually held early in the morning as a breakfast meeting, at noon as a luncheon, or immediately after working hours with light food and beverages. The keys to executive briefings, according to those who do them successfully, is to make the topic genuinely appealing to executives, to provide solid content in a succinct and professional way, to avoid any hint of selling, and to follow up afterwards in ways that directly connect to the issues of the briefing.

Advantages: When you do presentations and training workshops for businesses, hospitals, and nonprofit organizations, you will usually be paid unless you have offered to do the training without charge or are cosponsoring an event with another professional. Business presentations and training can range from $100 for an hour-long seminar for nonprofit volunteers to $4,000 for a daylong workshop for a group of managers or executives. Presenters and workshop leaders in business settings typically charge between $1,200 and $3,000 per day, while those speaking in the nonprofit sector may charge between $500 and $1,200 per day. Many brief lunch-and-learn events are not paid unless the company has approached you, although some speakers charge as much as $350 for a lunch-and-learn that has a clear benefit to the business. Unpaid speaking in a business setting can lead to much more paid speaking. Many speakers tell of giving an unpaid speech as a favor and have it lead directly to thousands of dollars' worth of speaking or training.

Sponsored presentations have several advantages. The sponsor usually publicizes the event because they want the exposure for the event and for their company or agency. As a speaker, you may be featured in a newsletter or newspaper that gives you exposure to far more people than those who actually attend the event. You may even be interviewed by a local television station. As a speaker, you benefit by the prestige and credibility of the sponsoring organization. The more you speak, the more you will be invited to speak elsewhere, especially when you speak at a well-publicized event.

Disadvantages: If your goal is not to become a professional speaker or trainer but only to attract more clients through your speaking, you can spend a lot of time preparing and speaking without much return unless you choose your engagements carefully.

National Trade and Professional Associations

Examples: American Association of Marriage and Family Therapists, American Psychological Association, National Association of Social Workers, Clinical Social Work Federation, American Counseling Association, American Psychiatric Association, and International Coaching Federation are examples to which therapists or coaches may belong, but every type of business has one or more national trade association that sponsors annual conferences. Consult the *Encyclopedia of Associations,* available in most public libraries, for descriptions of almost 23,000 associations.

Types of presentations: Presentations include keynote addresses and breakout sessions at national conferences and conventions. Continuing education courses may be offered through the national offices.

Advantages: To be a speaker at a national conference gives wide exposure and credibility. For a coach who wants to specialize in an industry, this can be an excellent venue to become known in a short time, especially among members of your professional niche.

Disadvantages: For large national associations, the competition is high to be selected as a speaker. Most speakers have become known at local and regional levels first, or have written a book that gives them high credibility. Keynote speeches are usually given by celebrity speakers or leaders in the field.

Classes, Workshops, and Seminars through Colleges, Universities, Adult Education, and Management Extension Programs

Examples: The most common example is teaching a workshop through the adult or continuing education division of a university or professional school. This is another version of a sponsored presentation. Many universities have extensive programs of adult education that are well publicized and well attended. Therapists may also teach a regular class as a part-time instructor at the local college or university, either to undergraduates or in one of the professional schools. Coaches may teach a class in a local business school. In addition, some states and counties have business development centers that offer continuing education events for businesses and entrepreneurs.

Advantages: The sponsorship of a college or university gives credibility and exposure. In many cases, their catalogs are widely circulated. Continuing education workshops are often proposed by the speaker, so you have latitude in designing a class that fits you and your interests. Most instructors are paid, although the rate may be fairly low given the amount of time required. In some cases, you may qualify for status as an adjunct faculty at a college or university.

Disadvantages: Preparing and teaching a class takes a lot of time.

Workshops and Classes That You Create and Lead Yourself

Examples: These can range from a one-hour free seminar held at your office to a weeklong workshop that you put on at a conference center at a charge of $500 or more.

The most common examples that therapists and coaches use to enhance their practice are:

- A free seminar or presentation of 1 to 2 hours, open to the public, often held at the therapist's or coach's office, on a topic of interest to prospective clients. Some therapy group practices offer a series of topics at regular intervals with different therapists in the practice presenting on topics of their own expertise. Many coaches offer a free teleclass, usually an hour long, on a topic related to their coaching specialty.
- An evening or weekend seminar or workshop for which participants pay anywhere from $10 to $30 (for an evening) to $150 for a weekend. Paid teleclasses are also offered by many coaches.

- A class or workshop series that meets weekly for 1 to 3 hours for 6 to 10 weeks for which participants pay $10 to $30 per session.

You will find detailed instructions on designing your own workshop, seminar, or teleclass in Chapter 10.

Advantages: Putting together your own seminar or workshop gives you the most control over the focus and design. A free evening seminar or teleclass can provide a service to the community as well as good exposure for you and can be fairly simple to plan and prepare. An ongoing class gives you a chance to develop a relationship with participants and gives them more opportunity to decide if they want to work with you as your client. This can be an effective way of marketing your services, while also providing a benefit to participants.

Disadvantages: Even a free evening seminar needs to be publicized in order to let people know about it. Longer, paid workshops and classes may take much more time to prepare and publicize. Low registration can result in your canceling the workshop after doing all the preparation, or teaching it with a small number of participants. If you invest in printing of brochures, mailings, or advertising, you could lose money if there is inadequate registration.

Professional, Academic, and Medical Audiences

Examples: Guest lectures, grand rounds, forums, and presentations of academic papers or research are possible venues.

Advantages: Being invited to give a presentation to academic or medical students and colleagues is an honor. In addition to adding to your professional reputation, presenting your research or cases can be intellectually stimulating and invigorating for you. If you are presenting on a topic related to your specialty, you may receive referrals as a result of your presentation.

Disadvantages: Academic and medical presentations require a high level of rigor and may need more time to prepare than most presentations. Depending on the audience, you may not receive any referrals as a result. Honoraria, if given, are usually modest.

❏ FINDING AUDIENCES FOR YOUR PRESENTATIONS

Sometimes invitations to speak come without any effort by the therapist or coach. Someone is looking for a speaker for their service club or Parent–Teacher Association (PTA), and knows or knows of the therapist or coach. They call and ask if the therapist or coach could do a program on stress management or dealing with change or whatever. It can be that easy. If you only want to speak once or twice a year and you are not particular about what kind of audience you address, you can let these kinds of invitations come without additional effort.

If you want more than an occasional opportunity to speak, unless you are already well known as a presenter, you will need to take some initiative. In this section, we describe the five main ways that you can get regular speaking opportunities. I recommend that you use a combination of the methods that fit your own temperament and speaking goals.

The five main ways to get speaking opportunities:

1. Develop a presentation and then tell everyone you meet that you are looking for organizations that might want a presentation on your topic.

2. Develop a presentation and then mail an introductory letter to appropriate contact people of organizations where you might speak.

3. Design a workshop or course on a topic, and then approach a nonprofit organization or educational institution proposing that the organization offer the workshop or course to their clientele or to the public, with you as the leader.

4. Design a workshop, seminar, or teleclass that you produce and offer yourself. You may do it by yourself or collaborate with one or more colleagues.

5.   Propose that you lead a workshop or breakout session as part of a professional or trade association conference.

In the next section we will describe in detail how to use each of these ways to arrange speaking opportunities. With each organization you contact, you should try to answer three questions for yourself:

1.   Is this organization a possible audience for your presentation? Part of this question is whether the program chairperson is interested in signing you up for a date, telling you when they expect to have an open date, or getting more information about you in order to decide whether to invite you to speak. But another part of the question is whether it sounds to you like their members would find your presentation interesting and helpful. You know your presentation better than they do, so you will have to weigh that for yourself. Do not rule out an organization only because initially they do not seem receptive. They may hear from many more speakers than they have openings. They may have had several therapists speak recently, or they may have had a coach or therapist give a speech that was poorly presented. In 6 to 12 months, they may be glad to hear from you again. If you are interested, ask whether it would be OK to check back with them in a few months to see whether they might be interested then; a different person may be chairing the program committee and may be very interested in you and your program.

2.   Are you interested in giving your presentation to this organization? Would giving a presentation to this group further your goals as a speaker? If your goal is to speak to as many people, anywhere, as you can, then every group that invites you may further your goals. But if you want to speak to groups that will likely lead to more referrals or further your reputation in a specialty, you may choose which groups are more likely to further these ends. If your initial goal is to build your skills and confidence as a speaker, you may not want to speak to a group where

you are likely to get a difficult or stony reception (for example, speaking to a group of employees who are *required* to attend your presentation on their own time over lunch or after hours).

3.   Are you willing and able to commit to the effort needed to do a good job with this presentation? You do not need to answer this question on the first phone call unless you have decided you want to accept an invitation to speak. Then the question of committing the effort to doing a good job becomes very important. It is human nature to think that we will have more time for things scheduled three or more months away than for things scheduled in the next two weeks. So we often commit to things in the distance without allowing for how much time they will take to prepare as the time draws nearer. We may also agree to adapting or customizing a presentation that will not take place for a few months. "I understand that you usually speak on communication between the sexes, but would you be willing to do a similar presentation on communication between the generations?" they ask. "Oh, sure, that shouldn't be that difficult," you respond. "I have lots of time to think and plan for that," you say to yourself. Then, as you begin to plan the presentation, several months from now, you may realize that this requires an entirely new presentation. Part of this question is about time and effort. Another part is about doing a good job. If this group's standards for speakers are higher than your current skill level, you need to decide if you will put in the practice to improve your skills so you can do a good job when the time comes.

❏ GETTING SPEAKING ENGAGEMENTS

Approach 1: Develop one or more presentations and then tell everyone you know that you are available to give presentations on that topic. Ask everyone you know about groups that might be interested in a presentation on the topic you have chosen. Ask your friends, neighbors, colleagues, people you do business with, and new people you meet. If you are a therapist, you will have to decide whether this is appropriate to bring up with your own clients. When you introduce yourself in business or networking settings, introduce yourself as a therapist and a speaker, or as a coach and workshop leader. Mention the topics that you speak about. If you see a sign in a restaurant that a service club meets there, ask for the name of the group's contact person. Then follow up on any and all leads.

If you are inexperienced as a speaker and need to get more practice and improve your speaking skills, you might not ask *everyone* you know about speaking opportunities. You may want to wait until you have more experience to ask key influential contacts or acquaintances about speaking recommendations. In the beginning, you may choose to focus on a few service clubs or religious organizations until you gain some confidence in your speaking skills. (Yes, it will happen!) Do not overlook organizations that you belong to. They might love to have you speak.

When you ask people about suggestions for groups that might be interested in your presentation, give them more information than just the title or topic. Tell them a little about your approach and what your presentation is designed to accomplish. Here's an example of what you might say: "I work with many women who are struggling with how to be good mothers and have meaningful careers. I've developed a presentation that I call: 'Dealing with the Special Stresses of Being a Woman in Business.' In the presentation I talk about the stresses and their effects. Women often feel there is something wrong with them, when the main problem is that so much is expected of them. I then help women look at their choices and how to have more control over them. It's a speech on empowerment—both of themselves and of their workplace. I'm wondering what groups you know that might be interested in a presentation like this. I'd be glad to do the presentation without charge because I enjoy doing this sort of thing, I like contributing to the community, and the exposure is good for me. What groups do you know that might like to have that kind of presentation?"

You might not say all that in one piece but as part of a give-and-take conversation where they asked you questions and you tell them more in response to their questions. Whatever your exact wording, be certain to include the title and specific topic of the talk, as well as at least one benefit that attendees will get from the talk.

When someone tells you about an organization that uses speakers, find out from them as much about the organization as you can. Ask them when and where the group meets, how many and what kinds of people are members, what kinds of programs they have had, and, most important, who you can contact for more information. Ideally you will get the name and phone number of the president or program chairperson. If not, find out the name and phone number of at least one member whom you can call for more information.

Before you call the contact person for the group, plan and practice how you will introduce yourself. You will be approaching them about speaking to their group, and they will form their first impression of you as a speaker by how you present yourself on the telephone. You do not want to fumble and stumble because you have not thought through what to say. So plan—and practice.

What is a good way to approach the contact person whose name you have been given? The following approach will work for most professional, community, and service organizations.

The first step is to call the phone number you have. If you found the listing in the newspaper, you may only have a phone number. If you get the person's voice mail, leave a message along these lines: "Hello, my name is _____ and my phone number is _____. I'm calling to find out who is in charge of arranging programs for the _____ (organization). I am a psychotherapist (or life coach) in the area specializing in _____. I have a program (or presentation) on _____ and would like to talk further about whether this would be of interest to your members. I'd appreciate your giving me a call with the name and number of the person I should talk to. My office number is _____ or you can call me at home in the evening at _____. Again, my name is _____ (spell it if it is anything but the most familiar of names)."

If you reach a person instead of their voice mail, you would say the same thing, except the part about having them call you back.

Notice that you give your name and phone number early in the message, and then you repeat them at the end, spelling your name if there could be any difficulty understanding it. The reason for giving your phone number early in the message is so that the person will not need to listen again to the entire message if they do not get your phone number the first time they listen. Speak slowly when you give your phone number because people cannot write as fast as most of us usually speak.

After you have determined that you are talking with the person who arranges programs for the organization, offer to tell them a little about your program on the phone or to send them a description of the program and yourself. Say something like: "I'd be glad to tell you a little about the program I have in mind, if this is a convenient time to talk. Or I can send you a brief description about the program and myself." In most cases, it's simpler to tell them about the program on the phone, so you may want to make it clear that this is your preference. Some advantages of talking before you send printed materials are that you may find out they are booked for the next year or that they use only a certain kind of program. You will learn more about what they are looking for so you can slant your program to fit their needs. You'll also have a chance to engage the person and let them get a feel for you. Even if it is not a convenient time for them to talk, you could arrange a time to call them back or for them to call you.

If they agree to talk rather than have you send them information, give the person a one-minute introduction to yourself and your possible topics. For example: "I'm a psychotherapist here in Glendale. I do both individual and marriage counseling. I've developed a presentation on 'Dealing with Difficult People at Work and at Home.' I also have a presentation on 'What Men and Women Can Learn from One Another.'" Then ask: "Does either of these sound like a topic that might interest your group?"

What you want to do now is learn more about the organization's program needs. There are several reasons for this. First, you want to make sure this is an organization you want to speak to—that its membership includes prospective clients, and that you and your topic are a good fit. The easiest way to learn more is to ask: "What kinds of programs do you consider for your organization?" As the person responds, you can ask more questions for clarification, such as these: "How many members do you have at a typical meeting? How long is the program portion? What are some other programs you've had?" Ask enough questions to find out if you and they are interested and to explain more about how your program would fit. You may only need to change the title a bit to make it a better fit.

Remember this: You are not trying to get them to let you speak, but rather you are telling them about a program you can offer. You are exploring whether this is a good fit. At this point, you are not committing to give a program. You do not need to *say* that, but you need to *remember* it so you won't feel stuck if you decide this is not a good fit for you. At the same time, present yourself positively. Do not be like the child selling candy door to door for his school who begins with: "You don't want to buy any candy, do you?" If you are too hesitant or cautious in your initial approach, you may encourage a less positive response.

Program chairpersons are usually not only concerned with getting a good topic, but also with getting a good presenter. They will want to know that you will not bore everyone to death and that you will not use the forum inappropriately to sell something.

Here are some ways to deal with these concerns: Be yourself and be engaging on the phone. People will form much of their impression of you in the first few minutes.

If possible, mention other presentations or public speaking you have done and positive responses you've had. For example: "I've given different versions of this talk several times. Last month I spoke to _____ on _____ and had a very positive response."

Mention that you make each presentation interesting and enjoyable. For example: "I always make sure that people have something they can take away from my presentations. I want them to learn something but I also want them to enjoy it." That you are concerned about content *and* enjoyment will reassure most program chairpersons.

Offer to send them some background material, even if they do not ask for it. This can be a letter telling more about yourself and your topic.

See the sample letter that follows. As you gain more experience, you may include more information, such as a brief biographical sheet, a list of your topics, news releases, thank-you letters from organizations where you have spoken, a photograph, a brochure, and copies of articles by you or about you.

If someone you know is active in an organization where you would like to speak, ask them if they would be willing to suggest you as a possible speaker to the president or program chairperson. A referral always makes your approach easier than calling or writing without introduction, so don't hesitate to ask for this favor from people you know. All they need to say to the program chair is: "I know this person and think she would make an interesting program speaker for us. She'll be calling you to tell you more about what she might speak about."

Approach 2: Mail a description of your presentations, along with a cover letter, to contact persons at organizations that might use a presentation on your topic. If you want to speak to community and service organizations, you would send the letter to program chairpersons or presidents of the organizations. You may also send the description and letter to businesses, governmental agencies, and nonprofit organizations if the topic would be appropriate for staff training. You then follow up by phone to make sure the person received the mailing and to see whether the person wants to talk further about your giving a presentation to their organization.

This approach differs from the first approach in that you get a list of organizations and approach them by mail and phone instead of relying on suggestions from people you meet. In most other ways, the methods are the same. The most effective method is to use both approaches.

Where do you find lists of organizations that use speakers?

- Look in the local newspaper for listings of meetings and events. The listings usually give the meeting information and a phone number for more information. Because these listings are usually for the current day or week, check at least a month of listings. Make it a habit to check these listings from now on to stay up to date with new organizations. Soon you may be speaking to some of these organizations.

- Ask at the reference desk of your local library for a directory of local community organizations. Reference librarians can help you find things you did not even know you should ask about.
- Call your local chamber of commerce. Ask for a directory of organizations. If you are interested in speaking to businesses, ask if they have a directory of local businesses. Often they have a directory of their members and also a directory of the larger businesses in the area. Usually there is a modest charge to buy these directories. You may also find them at the public library reference desk.
- Look in the Yellow Pages under "Associations" and under "Clubs and Organizations." Also check listings under "Social Service Organizations." You may be directed to "See also Athletic Organizations; Business and Trade Associations; Chambers of Commerce; Fraternal Organizations; Labor Organizations; Professional Organizations; Religious Organizations; Women's Organizations; Youth Organizations."
- Do an Internet search in Google or Yahoo! using words and phrases such as "associations," "clubs," "non-profit organizations," and "professional associations." Be sure to include the name of your city, town, or state in the search to limit the search to your region. Check under "Clubs," "Associations," or "meetings" on community Internet directories such as Citysearch (www.citysearch.com).
- If you want to approach businesses, agencies, and nonprofit organizations to offer a training workshop, try to get the names of the human resources director, the director of training, or the executive director if the organization is small.

Once you have a listing and a phone number, call to find out to whom you should send your information. Even if the directory listing includes a name and address, call to make sure it is current. If you are calling a business and do not have an individual's name, ask for the human resources department.

When calling, use the same introduction described in Approach 1. If you talk with the people in charge of programs and they ask you to send them more information, send them a letter describing your presentation and your background. You can use the sample letter in this chapter as a guide. If you have the time, interest, and skills, create a simple one-page description of your program, your background, and testimonials from previous speaking engagements. Professional speakers refer to these as *one-sheeters* and often print on both sides so they can include a photograph and a list of groups they have addressed.

If you do not have any testimonials yet from previous speaking, ask two or three colleagues or friends for a two-sentence quote about your knowledge of the topic, your professionalism, and your ability to speak in an engaging way. For example: "Dr. Jim Smith speaks clearly and engagingly about the causes and treatment of depression in children. He is the most knowledgeable person I know on the topic and one of the most skilled clinicians around." Create the sheet in a word processing or desktop publishing program such as Microsoft Word or Publisher, and print it on a color printer. This certainly is not necessary, but color printing gets people's attention and a simple one-sheeter conveys professionalism and gives people a quick summary of you and your program.

Do not assume that mailing the letter and one-sheeter to the right person is enough. People are busy and letters are laid aside. Many speakers tell of mailing out dozens of letters and not receiving a single response. The key is to follow up by phone until you make contact with a live person. If you get their voice mail, leave a message explaining why you are calling. But if they do not return your call, try them again in a week or two. If you would like to speak to their organization, do not give up until they either offer you a date to speak or tell you they are not interested. Persistence is the key. If you believe that you have a helpful, informative presentation, you are providing a service by making sure they know about you. As long as you are courteous and respectful, most people will appreciate and respect you for being persistent.

Approach 3: Design a workshop or course on a topic, and then approach a non-profit organization or educational institution proposing that the organization offer the workshop or course to their clientele or to the public with you as the leader. One variation of this approach is to design a class to be offered through the adult-education program of a local college or university. Duke University, for example, has an extensive adult and continuing education program with classes on everything from stress management to leadership development. They publish an extensive catalog, including the biographies of all their instructors.

If you are interested in teaching a class in your local adult-education program, call the schools in your area that offer adult education to find out the procedure. They often have a form for you to complete, outlining the class, the audience, and your background for teaching it. They may be looking for new classes and might welcome your suggestions.

Another variation is to propose a workshop series to be offered as an outreach program for a nonprofit organization. One of the most effective examples of this was developed by Debra Vajcner, a licensed marriage and family therapist in California. She approached a local substance-abuse recovery program about doing a series of workshops for family and friends of substance abusers. She designed classes of 10 weeks long that would meet once a week for $1^1/_2$ hours. The topics included panic and anxiety recovery, healing your aloneness, parenting skills, anger management, assertiveness training, healthy relationship and communication skills, and ending codependency. She charged $10 per person per session. When one class series ended, she started another on the same topics. The agency did lots of publicity and marketing for their programs, including hers. But in addition, Debra did a simple 4-page newsletter that she mailed out every couple months to 200 clients, former workshop participants, and referral sources. People passed it on to their friends. The workshops kept getting new people, with 15 to 20 people most weeks, and Debra's practice stayed full. She found it was easier to attract clients from the repetition of an ongoing class than from a single speaking engagement. People have time to develop trust and decide that you are someone they want to work with, according to Debra. As a therapist, she also found that speaking to a group of people with an identified need or problem (families and friends of substance abusers) is more likely to lead to more new clients than speaking to a general community group such as Lions or the PTA.

Workshops put on in conjunction with another organization can be as simple as a seminar at your local public library or YMCA. These seminars are typically offered at no charge or at a modest fee to the public or to their members. The advantage of a cosponsored workshop or seminar is that you get credibility from being associated with an organization such as the public library, the YMCA, a religious organization, or a local hospital. You may also get help with publicizing the event in their organization and the community.

You can arrange cosponsored workshops or seminars in one of two ways:

1. Find an organization that already offers workshops or seminars, and ask them how you can submit a proposal to do a workshop. They may have an application form or they may ask you to write a letter telling them what you would like to do.

2. Identify an organization that you believe would benefit by offering your workshop to their members, customers, or the community. Inquire with the organization about who is in charge of community outreach events. Call the person, introduce yourself, and tell them you would like to send them a proposal for a community outreach seminar. Send them a letter describing the seminar or workshop you would like to offer, including the benefits that people would get by attending and why you are qualified to lead the workshop. Follow up by phone after sending the letter to explore whether they are interested in offering the workshop and what questions they may have.

Many nonprofit organizations have speaker bureaus through which they offer programs to the community. In addition to their own staff, they often use people from the community to give these programs. A hospital or treatment center may be interested in offering programs on health and mental health issues. If you are a coach, you may get their interest by suggesting programs on life balance, personal goal setting, or getting organized. Programs that are offered through a speaker bureau are usually single events of 20 minutes to 2 hours and are usually presented to a group, club, school, or organization that requests a speaker for their event.

The advantage of being part of a speaker bureau is that you get credibility by your association with the nonprofit organization. The speaker bureau will usually handle all the arrangements, including publicity. The disadvantage is that you may be perceived as a representative of the nonprofit organization instead of as a person who can offer your own services.

Approach 4: Design a workshop or seminar that you produce and offer yourself. In the previous approaches, you designed the workshop and proposed it to be offered through an adult education program, a nonprofit organization's speaker bureau, or at a business. The difference in this approach is that you design the workshop *and* do all the publicizing and mailings to attract the participants. You also arrange for a space to hold the event. See Chapter 10 for a detailed discussion of how to design and produce your own workshops.

Approach 5: Propose that you lead a workshop as a continuing education event for association members or as an offering at a professional or trade association conference. Most professional associations offer continuing education events for their members, and most professions require a certain number of continuing education courses every year to remain licensed or certified. Sometimes these events are offered in connection with conferences, and we will discuss these shortly. Most associations also sponsor seminars and workshops on an occasional or ongoing basis. Some workshops are offered for a modest fee or none at all, as a benefit of association membership. Other workshops, especially daylong events, are a source of income for the association. Someone leads every one of those workshops, and most of the time the leader is not part of the association staff, but a professional who designs and leads the workshop and receives a fee for doing so. The fees may range from nothing to an amount comparable to an hourly therapy or coaching rate.

How do you get started leading association workshops?

First, identify associations in your area and find out what kinds of workshops they offer. Start with associations of which you or a colleague is a member. Some associations keep calendars and databases of continuing education offerings. Look over them to see what is being offered. Ask accountants, attorneys, dentists, physicians, chiropractors, realtors, nurses, and teachers what continuing education workshops are offered in their fields. Explain that you are exploring whether you, as a therapist or coach, might offer a workshop on your topic of interest to a professional group in their field. Be clear that you are asking for information, not that you are trying to get them to set something up for you. Most will be glad to give you ideas and contacts with which to follow up.

Next, make exploratory phone calls to the leads you have, introducing yourself and telling them about your interest in leading a workshop for them. Then, as in earlier examples, ask them what they are interested in. Find out what they need or wish they could offer. Be sure to find out the process for proposing a workshop. Ask about the budget for workshop leaders (asking what the budget is sounds easier to ask than how much they pay their leaders.).

Finally, write a proposal for the workshops that sound most appealing to you. The more organized and complete your proposal sounds, the more likely your workshop will be approved. Look over and follow the guidelines below for how to respond to Requests for Proposals (RFPs), since the same principals apply. Keep following up if you sense your proposal is a good fit. Be sure to include a description of your background and experience that makes you qualified to lead the workshop, as well as testimonials if possible.

Workshops held in conjunction with conferences can vary in length from a 60 or 90-minute breakout session (people "break out" from the main plenary meeting into smaller group sessions) to daylong workshops that may be the main purpose of the conference. Some conferences also sponsor preconference workshops, which are typically 1- or 2-day optional workshops before the conference. Sometimes the preconference workshops offer an opportunity for participants to receive training for a certification, to learn new techniques or methodologies, or to study with a well-known practitioner in the field.

Workshops at conferences are usually chosen from proposals submitted by people who want to lead a workshop at that conference. About a year before the conference, professional associations advertise and send out Requests for Proposals (RFPs) for workshops or breakout sessions at their conferences. Usually, the RFPs describe what you need to submit as a proposal for a workshop session.

Responding to Conference Requests for Proposals (RFPs)

Read the RFP carefully and follow the instructions concerning format, length, and information to be included. If it says, "No more than two pages in length," do not send them more. If they say, "include a 250-word biography," do not send your curriculum vitae.

- Make sure your workshop proposal clearly fits the theme or categories for the conference. If the conference theme is "Walking Together into the Future," find a way to include collaboration or community and a future direction in your workshop focus. This will significantly increase the likelihood that your workshop proposal will be accepted.
- Make your learning objectives practical, clear, and appealing for the intended audience. Do not make them general or vague. For example, if the conference is for social workers, instead of "Participants will learn techniques for dealing with stress," write, "Participants will learn 5 stress management techniques to use in their daily work with clients." If a personal coach is proposing a workshop for a nurse's conference: instead of "Participants will learn techniques for self-care," write, "Participants will learn and practice three key self-care skills for nurses to counteract compassion fatigue."

- Come up with a title that will get people's attention and make them want to know more. Look at the section on Titles in Chapter 3 for ideas.
- Do not be modest, but avoid hype. Try to find the zone where you communicate confidence without exaggerating.
- Write the description using active verbs and nontechnical language. Ask a good writer to read over your RFP and suggest ways to make it clearer and more appealing.

Approach 6: Propose a workshop or seminar to a professional seminar company. Professional seminar companies are businesses that produce and market workshops and seminars, usually to business and professional audiences. You may already receive mailings from some of them. If you are a good presenter with an idea, and preferably an outline, for a workshop or seminar, you could approach a professional seminar company to see if they would be interested in your developing the seminar for them. Another option is to see if they need presenters for workshops they have already developed.

The advantage of working with a professional seminar company is that they do all the marketing, and they do it well. You would get lots of exposure and experience as a presenter. This type of seminar leadership can be one path toward becoming a professional speaker.

The disadvantages are that professional seminar companies generally do not pay as much as you might make in other ways ($200 to $400 per day is common). The schedule is often grueling, with a seminar a day in different cities for several days in a row. If you are presenting a seminar for a public seminar company, you cannot promote your own business or services, although you will naturally make contacts and get exposure.

If you are interested in pursuing doing workshops with a professional seminar company, call some of the seminar companies listed in the Resources section. Tell them you are a speaker and workshop leader with a seminar you would like to propose. If your topic fits the types of seminars they do, they will probably ask you to send them an outline with your credentials.

Even before you do that, you might want to contact seminar leaders you see listed in professional seminar flyers. Tell them you are considering approaching the company about doing a seminar. Ask them about their experiences working with the company.

❏ DECIDING ON YOUR APPROACH

Which of these approaches are best for you depends on several factors:

- Why do you want to do presentations and what results are you looking for? Do you want to become better known and generate more referrals, or do you want to make money from speaking itself? Do you want to become known primarily among professional colleagues or do you hope to become better known among prospective clients?
- How much time do you want to devote to speaking and to lining up speaking engagements? Do you want speaking and presentations to be a significant part of your work, or do you want to speak only enough to generate a few more referrals?
- How comfortable are you with networking and making phone calls to promote yourself and your speaking?
- How specialized are your speaking topics and your practice specialties? Would they appeal to a general audience, or do they only appeal to a limited audience?
- What is your style of speaking and how well do you engage and keep an audience's attention and interest? Can you make and keep a connection with an audience or do you need to develop those skills?
- What kind and size community do you live in, and how many groups, companies, and nonprofits might use or sponsor speakers?
- Are you already established in the community or in your specialty, or are you "starting from scratch" in a new location or in your field or specialty?

- Do you want to become better known in your local geographical area, or do you want to become known across a larger geographical area?

If you are primarily interested in generating a few more referrals in your own community and do not plan to devote large amounts of time to speaking, telling people you are available to speak and sending letters to local organization should meet your needs. If you are new to the community and want to build a practice from scratch, you will need to be more aggressive in lining up as many presentations and making as many contacts as possible. If you want to earn additional income from speaking, in addition to getting referrals, you will need to hone your speaking skills and design presentations that organizations are willing to pay for. The quickest way to start making money from speaking is by doing training events for businesses or nonprofit organizations and to do sponsored presentations. Chapter 10 goes into more detail on doing workshops and training.

❏ WHAT ARE YOU LOOKING FOR IN AN AUDIENCE?

If you are just starting as a speaker, you may be willing to speak to any audience that will have you. In the beginning, if you have time available, speaking to as many groups as you can is a good way to improve your speaking skills and to get exposure that can lead to other speaking invitations.

If you do not have time to speak to many different audiences and want to focus your efforts on audiences that may lead to referrals, what should you do? The answer is to look for audiences containing people who could become clients and people who might refer prospective clients to you.

The first step is to clarify who your prospective clients and referral sources are. Here are some questions to ask yourself that can help identify the kinds of groups you may want to seek out. I have included some examples to help stimulate your thinking.

1. Who are your current or prospective clients? Who are they in terms of occupation, age group, geographical location, gender, and so on? What groups do your current or prospective clients belong to? If you do not yet have clients, think about the kinds of people you want to develop as clients, that you enjoy working with and work with best.

2. Who do you know or have contacts with? What groups and organizations do they belong to? Do they have regular meetings or conferences with speakers?

3. Who makes referrals to you or could make referrals to you? What groups and organizations do they belong to?

4. With which individuals or categories of people would you like to develop a professional relationship? To which groups and organizations do they belong?

EXAMPLE 4.1. If You Are a Therapist

Current or prospective clients: Women between ages of 20 and 50; women with weight loss and eating issues; women and men going through divorces; women facing "empty nest" phase of life; many clients who are in scientific and health care–related careers. *Possible groups:* Health and fitness clubs and spas; singles groups; church groups; business and professional groups; women's centers and groups; professional organizations for people in technical or health care fields.

Who do you know or have contacts with? Neighbors; friends; coworkers; family members; suppliers; customers; members of church or religious organization; people I do business with; people I know from other organizations I participate in.

What groups do they belong to that may use speakers?: Several civic and professional organizations; the mental health association; several trade associations. I am not sure which ones use speakers, but I can ask.

Who makes referrals to you?: Family physician; ministers and rabbis; former supervisors at mental health center; other therapists who do not work with eating disorders; therapists who know me from professional associations who tend not to have many openings; former clients; an EAP that serves some of the technical companies nearby.

Who else could make referrals?: Other physicians; other ministers and rabbis; other therapists with whom I have not kept in touch; therapists who do not know about my work with eating and weight-loss issues; male therapists to whom I refer clients; therapists who are nearing retirement; nutritionists who do not have a therapy background; other EAPs who do not know about me.

What groups and organizations do they belong to?: Mental health-center staffs; EAP staffs; local or state professional associations for psychologists, psychiatrists, clinical social workers, marriage and family therapists, professional counselors, and dieticians/nutritionists; ministerial associations; churches and synagogues; medical practices.

Topic examples: The therapist could develop a presentation or workshop for a general audience, including health and fitness spas, on a topic like "Developing a Healthy Body Image" or "The Mental Game of Staying Healthy" or "Navigating the Stages of Life for Adult Women." The therapist might develop a presentation for professional organizations and EAP staffs on a topic like "What Most Professionals Don't Know About Eating Disorders, But Should" or "Helping Women Develop a Healthy Body Image."

EXAMPLE 4.2. If You Are a Coach

Current or prospective clients: Men and women; ages 30–55 (most are 35–50); professionals (physicians, dentists, lawyers, chiropractors); self-employed entrepreneurs; owners of family businesses; professional sales people in technical, financial services, and pharmaceutical fields. Most have been in local geographical area but I want to expand beyond local area. Clients tend to want to work on improving personal and sales performance, achieving more balance, finding more satisfaction, and staying focused. Some people are rethinking their career path and direction. Some also want to work on improving interpersonal effectiveness and "emotional intelligence."

Possible groups: Professional associations; civic and community organizations; sales and marketing associations; chamber of commerce; boards of directors of nonprofit organizations; country clubs; alumni associations; business school gatherings; business networking organizations such as Business Networking International, The Executive Committee, and The Alternate Board.

Who do you know or have contacts with?: Neighbors; friends; coworkers; family members; people I do business with; school, college, and graduate school classmates; coworkers in former companies or who have gone to work in other organizations; my own physician, dentist, attorney, chiropractor, and other professionals; people on the boards of nonprofits I am involved in.

Who makes referrals to you?: Current and former clients; an attorney who works with many family businesses; a dean at the medical school; members of my business network; other coaches who have different specialties than mine; coaches to whom I have referred clients when I felt they would be a better fit; Vice President of sales for a corporation where two of my clients are salespeople; people who have heard me speak.

Who else could make referrals?: Other attorneys who work with businesses and professional practices; other sales executives who want to help develop their sales staff; financial planners and advisers who work with the types of client I do; executive recruiters who help place high level professionals and salespeople.

What groups and organizations do they belong to?: Professional and business associations such as sales and marketing executives; economic development councils; financial-planning trade associations; executive-recruiting trade associations. I need to ask the people I know about organizations that would be good for making presentations.

Topic example: Coaches could start with local associations but then expand to state and regional organizations and trade associations. They might develop a presentation on a topic like "Emotional Intelligence for Smart People" or "High Performance Doesn't Have to Mean High Stress" or "What to Do When There's Not Enough Time to Do Everything."

❏ SAMPLE LETTERS

Letter to Program Chairperson from a Therapist

This would be on your letterhead using a standard letter format.

[Date]

Ms. Margaret Smith
321 Any Street
Your City, NY 22222

Dear Ms. Smith:

I am a psychologist in private practice specializing in women and work issues.

I am writing to see if the University Women's Association would be interested in a presentation on "What Men and Women Can Learn from One Another" or one on "Dealing with the Stresses of Women at Work."

In the first presentation I explore, in a direct but entertaining way, the very real differences between women and men. I then talk about ways we can support each other from our strengths.

In the second presentation I explore some of the particular stresses that women face in today's work climate, and then suggest ways we can exercise our power to change some of the norms. My doctoral research was on stress among women in academic settings.

I deal with the complexities of these issues and I don't oversimplify the topics. At the same time, I take a positive approach and offer some hopeful options. I have had very positive feedback from audiences in the past.

If either of these topics sounds like it might fit as one of your programs, I would be glad to tell you more about the content and my experience as a speaker. I can tailor a presentation to meet your needs—anything from a 20-minute talk to a daylong workshop.

I'd like a chance to talk with you directly, so I will call you in the next week or so. If you have questions in the meantime, give me a call at [your telephone number].

Sincerely,

[Your Name, degree]

Letter to Program Chairperson from a Coach

This would be on your letterhead using a standard letter format.

[Date]

Ms. Margaret Smith
321 Any Street
Your City, NY 22222

Dear Ms. Smith:

I am a personal and professional coach who specializes in women and work issues. My clients tend to be successful women who want to achieve a higher level of performance, satisfaction, and balance in their lives.

I am writing to see if the University Women's Association would be interested in a presentation on "The Hidden Power of Conflict" or one on "Using Your Intuition to Enhance Your Life."

In the first presentation I explore how conflict, when faced and embraced, can lead to changes we previously thought were impossible. In a direct but entertaining way, I look at how we tend to deal with conflict. Then I present a step-by-step model for approaching conflict constructively.

In the second presentation I explore what intuition is, what happens when we ignore it, how to develop it, and how we can use intuition to enhance our lives. I end with some stories of how ordinary people have used intuition to make significant breakthroughs in their lives.

I deal with the complexities of these topics and I don't over-simplify the issues. At the same time, I take a positive approach and offer some hopeful options. I have had very positive feedback from audiences in the past.

If either of these topics sounds like it might fit as one of your programs, I would be glad to tell you more about the content and my experience as a speaker. I can tailor a presentation to meet your needs—anything from a 20-minute talk to a day-long workshop.

I'd like a chance to talk with you directly, so I will call you in the next week or so. If you have questions in the meantime, give me a call at [your telephone number].

Sincerely,

[Your Name]
Personal & Business Coach

Letter Offering In-service Training

This would be on your letterhead using a standard letter format.

[Date]

Betty Doe, M.D.
All Specialties Medical Associates
321 Any Street
Your Town, NY 11111

Dear Dr. Doe:

I am psychologist in private practice specializing in women, couples, and work issues. I am writing to offer an in-service work-shop at no charge for your staff in any of these areas:

- Communicating Care: Keys to Patient Communication

- Self-Care for Caregivers
- Understanding and Supporting the Grieving Patient
- Managing Stress in a Time of Managed Care

Because there are such high demands on medical staffs, I am offering an in-service workshop on one of these topics as part of my outreach to the community. The in-service workshops are usually 60 to 90 minutes long and can be given at your office site or at my office, whichever works better for you. I would be happy to tailor the workshop to meet your needs.

My approach is to make the workshops interactive, lively, and fun, while making sure participants leave with insights they can start applying immediately. Each time I do in-service workshops with medical office staffs, the participants and physicians report that they not only benefit individually, but that the staff morale and mood improve as well.

Enclosed is a short biographical sketch and description of my professional practice. As you can see, I have broad experience in medical and hospital settings as well as family service agencies. I am also trained and experienced in doing critical incident debriefings.

I will call your office next week to answer any questions you may have and to see whether I might come by and meet you. In the meantime, if you have particular questions about the in-service offerings, give me a call at [your telephone number].

Sincerely,

[Your Name, degree]

❏ PLACES WHERE THERAPISTS AND COACHES MAY SPEAK

The following list of organizations that could be appropriate for coaches and therapists is intended to trigger your thinking about possible groups for your presentation. As you look through the list, make notes of which ones appeal to you and jot down the names of people you could talk with about different types of groups.

Educational Programs and Conferences

- Adult education programs
- Career conferences (you could speak on making career choices, dealing with career transition, or handling the stress of job hunting, for example)
- Community colleges
- Speaker bureaus
- Conferences for people in your region who are prospective clients or referral source: (for therapists these may include teachers, health professionals, social service providers, clergy, funeral directors, etc. For coaches, these may include many of these as well as entrepreneurs, professionals of all types, executives, managers, salespersons and sales executives, human resource professionals, other coaches, etc.)
- Continuing education programs through colleges, universities, professional schools, and professional associations
- Health education programs sponsored by public or private organizations
- Clinical and professional organizations with in-service opportunities
- Alcohol and drug treatment programs
- College and university counseling centers
- Employee assistance programs (EAPs)
- Health maintenance organizations (HMOs)
- Hospices
- Hospitals
- Medical societies
- Mental health and community counseling centers
- Nonprofit organizations such as the Red Cross, etc.
- Public libraries
- Public and private schools
- Social service agencies
- Telephone hotlines

Businesses and Business Organizations

- Company-sponsored training and events
- Bar associations
- Business and professional women's associations
- Business and professional group associations, such as real estate agents, merchants, American Society for Training and Development (ASTD), sales and marketing executives, public relations associations, advertising clubs, etc.
- Business employees (contact the human resources department to see if they would be interested in a lunch-and-learn seminar)
- Chambers of commerce, which often have business expos and breakfast meetings that use speakers
- Networking organizations
- Athletic and health clubs
- Trade shows and expos
- Cruise ships

Civic and Community Groups

- Civic clubs such as Kiwanis, Lions, Civitan, Rotary
- Churches and synagogues, including boards, special classes, training, men's and women's groups
- Neighborhood associations
- Public libraries (they often cosponsor speeches that have a community interest)
- PTAs, including special parents' issues groups (public and private schools)
- Alumni associations

Self-help Organizations and Programs

- Health education organizations such as the American Cancer Society, American Lung Association, American Diabetes

Association, Association for Retarded Citizens (ARC), Muscular Dystrophy Association, etc.
- Mental health associations
- Parents Without Partners and other singles' organizations
- Retired persons' associations and senior citizen groups
- Self-help groups such as job-hunting support groups, anxiety support groups, chronic disease support groups

WORKSHEET 4.1. Possible Audiences

The purpose of this worksheet is to help you expand your ideas about possible audiences for your speeches. Approach it with an attitude of brainstorming and discovery. Adapt the questions to fit your situation. You will not know the answers to all the questions, so you may need to put down everything you can, including guesses, and then do more research later.

Instructions:

1. On a separate sheet, make a list of your current and recent clients, or refer to your client roster.
2. List their occupations/employers and their age groups (teens, 20s, 30s, etc.), gender, and geographical locations of home and work.
3. List the groups and organizations to which your current clients might belong. Be sure to include the person's employing organization as one of the groups in all of the following questions. (I realize that a therapist may not want to speak to organizations where your clients are members, but this exercise can help you identify groups of people similar to your clients.)
4. List other kinds of clients you would like to reach. What types of people do you enjoy working with? What kinds of people are you especially effective with?
5. Make a list of everyone who makes referrals to you, including their role or relationship to you (colleague, classmate, physician, minister or rabbi, hospital social workers, EAP staff, etc.).
6. List the organizations to which they might belong (including employers).
7. Who else could make referrals to you? List people in similar categories to those you have listed above or categories of referral sources that you have not cultivated.
8. What groups do they belong to (including employers)?
9. List everyone you know or have contacts with in any of the organizations where you may want to speak.

10. What groups and organizations do you belong to or qualify for? Which ones have regular meetings or conferences with speakers?

11. What regional or national conferences do you receive mailings for? At which of them would you be interested in speaking or leading a breakout session?

12. What organizations offer continuing education events in your area?

    Colleges or universities:

    Community colleges:

    Local school systems:

    Public libraries:

13. What organizations in your area may provide in-service workshops for their staff?

14. What organizations that might be good audiences for you are listed in the Yellow Pages under "Associations," "Clubs," "Organizations," "Professional Organizations," and "Social Service Organizations"?

WORKSHEET 4.2. Speech-Tracking Sheet

This form can be used to keep track of information about upcoming speaking engagements.

On a photocopy, fill in the initial information and then add information as you take action or receive more details. This form can serve as a checklist for getting information from the organization where you will be speaking and for following through with details of your actions.

Name of organization: _____

Address: _____

_____

Contact person: _____

Work phone: _____   Home phone: _____

Fax: _____   Cellular phone: _____

Day, date, and time of speech: _____

Location: _____

Topic: _____

Title: _____

Pre-speech questionnaire sent? _____

Pre-speech questionnaire received? _____

Biographical and publicity information sent? _____

News release written? _____

News releases sent? _____

To whom? _____

Follow-up phone calls to media? _____

Name of person who will introduce me? _____

Phone:_____   Fax: _____

Introducer contacted?_____

Introduction sent? _____

WORKSHEET 4.3. Brief Pre-Speech Questionnaire

This form can be mailed, e-mailed, or faxed to the contact person at the organization where you will be speaking.

Fill in the information that you already know, including your own contact information. Set the date for return well in advance of the speech so you can send them another if they lose it. Mail, e-mail, or fax it to the organization's contact person. Follow up with a phone call if you do not receive it by the expected date. You may also choose to follow up by phone for more details and explanations about their responses.

From _____ **[Your name]**

I am preparing for my presentation to your group on _____ and need some additional information. Please complete the missing information and double-check everything else. Fax, e-mail, or mail the completed form to me no later than _____.

My fax is: _____.

My mailing address is: _____

My e-mail address is: _____

If you have questions, call me at_____

Presentation topic and/or title: _____

Day and date: _____

Full name of organization or conference: _____

Exact location where speech will take place: _____

Starting time of speech:_____

Ending time of speech: _____

When will people arrive? _____

Expected number in the audience?_____

Average age or age range: _____

Gender: _____ % male _____ % female

Will it be possible to answer questions as part of the time allotted?

_____

Who will introduce me?_____

Name: _____

Phone: _____

If you have any questions, please call or e-mail me.

WORKSHEET 4.4. Full Length Pre-Speech Questionnaire

Purpose: This form is an extended version of the Brief Pre-speech Questionnaire and is intended for major speeches to organizations with which you are not familiar. The full-length version probably asks for more information than you need for the typical speech you will give, but it is appropriate for a keynote address and can be invaluable in helping you customize your speech to the audience.

To use: Fill in the information that you already know, including your own contact information. Set the date for return well in advance of the speech so you can send them another if they lose it. Mail, e-mail, or fax it to the organization's contact person. Follow up with a phone call if you do not receive it by the expected date. You may also choose to follow up by phone for more details and explanations about their responses.

From _____ **[Your name]**

I am preparing for my presentation to your group on _____
and need some additional information. Please complete the missing information and double-check everything else. Fax, e-mail, or mail the completed form to me no later than _____.

My fax is: _____.

My mailing address is: _____

My e-mail address is: _____

If you have questions, call me at _____

Presentation topic and/or title: _____

Day and date: _____

Full name of organization or conference: _____

Exact location where speech will take place: _____

Starting time of speech: _____

Ending time of speech: _____

When will people arrive? _____

What takes place immediately before I speak? _____

What takes place after I speak? _____

Will it be possible to answer questions as part of the time allotted?

_____

Will there be other speakers on the program?_____

Name: _____   Topic: _____

Name: _____   Topic: _____

Where in the program does my presentation come?

Near the beginning:_____

Near the middle: _____

Near the end: _____

Who will introduce me?

Name: _____

Phone: _____

What is the overall purpose and/or theme of the meeting? _____

Appropriate dress for the presentation: _____

Formal: _____

Business attire:_____

Casual: _____

What have been some previous speakers and topics?_____

Without naming names, what have you liked and not liked about previous topics and speakers?_____

Information about the audience:

Expected number in the audience?_____

Age range: _____

Average age: _____

Gender: _____ % male _____ % female

Median educational level of audience:

_____ High school

_____ Some college

_____ College graduates

_____ Graduate degrees

What do members of the audience do for a living?_____

Can you give me the names of three people who will be in the audience that I might talk with in advance to gain more understanding about the audience and its needs?

Name: _____   Phone: _____

Name: _____   Phone: _____

Name: _____   Phone: _____

Room arrangements: _____

What is the approximate size of the room (dimensions or square footage)? _____

How will the chairs be arranged?

_____ Auditorium style in rows

_____ Classroom style at tables

_____ Banquet style at tables

_____ Other (describe:) _____

Will there be a head table?_____

Will there be a podium?_____

Will there be a microphone and public address system? _____

What audiovisual equipment will be available? _____

Background Information:

What are some examples of workplace problems or challenges faced by the audience in relation to my topic?_____

What are the major challenges and successes of your organization?

_____

Have there been any special events or news recently affecting your members that I should know about? (Major changes, cutbacks, relocations, mergers, breakthroughs, etc.) _____

Who should I contact if I have further questions?

Name: _____

Position:_____

Phone numbers: _____   Work: _____

Home:_____   Cell: _____

E-mail: _____

CHAPTER 5

Planning and Preparing Your Presentation

ONCE YOU HAVE IDENTIFIED the types of groups you want to speak to and some possible topics, you are ready to start developing your presentation. In the beginning, I recommend that you develop one speech that you can adapt to various audiences. By focusing on one speech, you can improve the content and delivery each time you give it, and you'll spend less time getting ready since you will not have to construct a new speech each time.

Preparing a speech invariably takes longer than one expects, so start work several weeks in advance if possible. You can give a better presentation when you have plenty of time to plan, prepare, and practice.

If you already have a presentation that you have given and want to give it again, skim this chapter for ideas or elements you may want to incorporate into your presentation.

❏ BUILDING A SPEECH FROM THE GROUND UP

Once you have a topic, follow this four-step process for putting together your presentation: (a) hunt; (b) gather; (c) arrange; (d) play, practice, and prune.

Step 1: Hunt—Do enough research to find and decide on the main point and subpoints of your presentation.

Step 2: Gather—Gather additional information, examples, arguments, and stories that relate to your topic *and* that help explain or support your points.

Step 3: Arrange—Arrange and rearrange the points, with examples and illustrations, until you have an order that makes sense and a flow that is easy to follow.

Step 4: Play, Practice, and Prune—Give your presentation aloud, first alone, and then with one or more colleagues or friends, focusing on becoming clear, comfortable, and connected with your audience. Play with the phrasing and with your movements. Prune anything that does not add to the overall impact.

The process of speech preparation is too complex and creative to always fit neatly into a series of sequential steps, but these steps can be a guide to help make manageable what may otherwise feel overwhelming. As you work on your presentation, you will probably find yourself looping back more than once to the first steps as you revise and refine your presentation. That is a normal part of the creative process

Let's walk through each of the steps.

❏ STEP 1: Hunt

One of the most common mistakes coaches and therapists make in planning presentations is to gather so much information that they could almost write a book about what they know. They find so many good points to make, and they are reluctant to part with any of them. At some level they know they have too much. At the same time, they may fear they will come across as not knowing enough. People in this position often become paralyzed when trying to decide what to include in their presentations. They do not realize that often the problem lies in their own conflict between wanting to be seen as effective and knowledgeable, and the limitations of a 20- or 30-minute speech. They may conclude that the problem is that they still do not have the "right" material or content, so they spend more time researching and obsessing about what to say.

How do you avoid this trap? Do enough, but only enough, research to decide on one main point and preferably no more than three subpoints that support your main point. You will use these points as a basis for gathering more material, but you will be looking for the specific material you need rather than researching everything possible on your topic. For now, your goal is to decide on your main and supporting points. Keeping your focus limited to these points will help you spend energy on the right material, rather than wasting time reading up on everything you can get your hands on.

The other key to avoiding the trap of too much material is this: Accept that you will finish every speech feeling that you did not cover the topic with the depth it needed. You will feel like you barely scratched the surface. You will wonder whether the audience thinks that was all you know about the topic. Eormation they may ever need to know on a subject. Speeches are not designed to present large amounts of information or knowledge. Reading is. Study is. If the audience members need or want more depth of information, you may suggest additional reading.

Remmormation they may ever need to know on a subject. Speeches are not designed to present large amounts of information or knowledge. Reading is. Study is. If the audience members need or want more depth of information, you may suggest additional reading.

Remember that the purpose of a presentation is not to tell the audience everything you know or that you would like them to know about the topic. The purpose of a presentation is usually *one* of the following: (a) to introduce the audience to a topic and give them some knowledge or a perspective that they lacked before; (b) to introduce the audience to one or more possible ways of dealing with a problem or situation in their lives; (c) to *inspire* or persuade the audience to do something new.

A typical length for presentations to clubs and organizations is 20 to 30 minutes. If you have three points, each one can only take about 5 minutes in a 20-minute speech or 7 to 8 minutes in a 30-minute speech. That is all the time you will have after allowing for your opening and closing remarks. You may have even less time if you also allow time for questions. In five minutes, you only have time to state your point, elaborate and explain briefly, give a couple of examples, tell one or two brief anecdotes, and then summarize or drive home the point. If you wrote the speech out, which I do not recommend, 5 minutes is less than one and a half double-spaced pages.

When you are beginning to prepare for a presentation, you can save yourself hours or days of time and frustration by doing only enough research to decide on your main and supporting points. As soon as you have up to three points that support your main point, stop doing general research and start looking for examples, stories, and illustrations about the points you have chosen.

A presentation should have one main point with up to three to five subpoints that support the main point. A workshop seems like an exception to the one-main-point rule, but that is because a workshop is actually a *series* of presentations on different, but related, topics.

If you ever listened to a speech and then afterward were confused about what the speaker was saying, the reason was probably that the speaker did not have one main point.

It is not enough that your speech be on *one subject*. If you give a speech on change or even dealing with change, you will not necessarily have one main point. Suppose your three points are (a) change is inevitable; (b) change can be exciting or scary; (c) think about how you deal with change. What is the overarching point that pulls all three points together? I do not see one. Neither would the audience. Yet many speakers string together points that seem related because they are on the same subject. Unfortunately the speech is not successful because it does not have a single unifying direction.

If your presentation has a single unifying direction, you will eventually be able to state its main point in one sentence. You may not know what the point will be when you start planning your speech. You may need to find or create a single point from the mix of points you want to make. You may try several different ways of approaching your topic and organizing your presentation before you find the one you want, but the one way of knowing whether you have a single unified direction for your speech is that you will be able to state the message in one sentence, and every subpoint will directly support that main point. Until you can state your topic in one sentence, you do not really know what your speech is about.

As you prepare your presentation, write down one major point that you would want to make in your presentation. Write it in the form of a complete sentence, not just a phrase. For example, if your topic is "Dealing with Change," one of your points might be: "Change is an inevitable part of life." Write it as a sentence that would make sense if you said it to an audience, not just as a note to yourself. Thus, write: "Change is an inevitable part of life" rather than "Change part of life" or "Change and life." Another example would be to write: "Change is scary to some people and exciting to others" rather than "Change scary to some, exciting to others."

Next, write down any other points you can think of that you might include in your presentation. This is a time for brainstorming. Do not spend much time on getting the exact wording as long as you use sentences. Get the meaning down right now. You may use all the points you write down. You may not use any of them. Perhaps one or more of the points will be part of your presentation, but you may revise and refine them before you find the point you want to make.

Here is my initial brainstorming list for the topic "Dealing with Change:"

- Change is an inevitable part of life.
- Change is scary to some people and exciting to others.
- How we view a particular change will depend, in part, on how we perceive it and whether we view the expected outcome as desirable.
- The less we know about what is likely to happen, the more threatening the change will probably be.
- Most people deal with change better when they don't feel they are dealing with it alone.
- We usually deal with change better when we have some sense of control over the outcome of a change.

- Change means the end of one thing and the beginning of something new.
- Something usually has to end for something new to begin.
- Between one ending and a new beginning is an "in between" phase that can be especially scary and chaotic.
- The change process follows a pattern that can be studied and understood.
- If we understand the change process, we will be better able to deal with it.

Using this list, how could I come up with one main point with supporting subpoints? Here are some options.

I could decide I want to focus on the value of understanding the stages of change. Using William Bridge's three stages of change (from his book *Transitions*), my main point could be: "We can deal with change better when we understand the stages it follows." Three supporting subpoints could be: (a) Change has three stages: an ending, an in-between, and a new beginning; (b) after an ending and before a new beginning is an in-between phase that can be especially scary and chaotic; (c) if we seem stuck in dealing with change, we may be avoiding an ending, rushing to a new beginning, or feeling lost in the in-between.

Another arrangement, using this example, would be to use the first subpoint as the main point: "Change has three stages: an ending, an in-between, and a new beginning." Subpoints (b) and (c) could be subpoints of this main point as well.

Yet another option for a main point could be: "How people deal with change will depend on how they perceive it and whether they want the expected outcomes." Three supporting subpoints could be: (a) People usually deal with change better when they have some sense of control or voice over the outcome of a change; (b) people usually deal with change better when they are kept informed about what to expect; (c) most people deal with change better when they don't feel like they are dealing with it alone.

A further example for a main point could be: "The most important factor in people dealing with change is for them to feel they are not alone." Supporting subpoints could be: (a) We can facilitate this by bringing people together regularly to talk and socialize; (b) we can facilitate this by listening to people and responding empathically; (c) we can facilitate this by making sure everybody is given up-to-date information about what is happening.

I hope it is clear from these examples that you can focus your presentation in a variety of directions, depending on what points seem most important and interesting for you and your audience. After you have brainstormed points that you may want to use in a presentation, ask yourself the following questions to further clarify your choosing:

- Which is the broadest point?
- Which will be most useful to my audience?
- Which will give them something they can apply?
- Which are most interesting, unique, or memorable?
- Which are different from what people commonly think, say, or believe?
- Which do I understand best or know the most about?
- Which am I most intrigued by?
- Which do I have examples and stories to illustrate?
- Which ones fit together to make one unified and cohesive point?

You may find that you have more points than you can use in one presentation. Some points will fit better with certain types of audiences, such as a group of parents or business professionals. Eventually you may choose to develop different points into "modules." You may develop several different "modules" or interchangeable components on ways to handle stress that you would use with different audiences. One point or module may be on handling stress at work. Another may be on handling stress in relationships. A third might be on handling the stress of aging or illness. Yet another may be on helping children handle stress. You might develop an introduction about what stress is that could fit almost any audience. Then, once you had developed these points into "sections" or "modules," you could quickly adapt a presentation on stress to different audiences by using the opening section on what stress is. You would plug in the "module" on handling stress that was most appropriate to the audience. You would then have four different speeches without four times the preparation. This "module method" can help as you do more presentations. For now, however, we will focus on developing one speech.

At this point, you may already know what your main and supporting points will be. As you go through the next steps of gathering examples, stories, and information, and rearranging the points, you may revise some of your subpoints and may even decide on a new main point. That is normal for most speakers. These revisions and fine-tunings will probably lead to a more effective presentation.

❏ STEP 2: Gather

Your goal at this stage is not to research your topic exhaustively but to find illustrations, examples, stories, explanations, analogies, statistics, and quotations to flesh out the points you have chosen to make. You will gather more material than you can use and will choose only the best and the most appropriate for your presentation.

One of the most overlooked and valuable resources for preparing a presentation is accessing what you already know about the topic—your experiences, your thinking, your stories, and your viewpoint. The Speech Preparation Worksheet at the end of this chapter is designed to help you draw on your own experience. Another strategy is to ask other people about their own experiences with the topic and what they would be most interested in knowing if they were in the audience.

Many professional speakers describe how they are always looking and listening for stories and examples to illustrate their speeches. When they are looking for examples, they notice them in the everyday events of their lives. If they do not watch for them, nothing relevant to their speeches ever happens. Professional speakers also emphasize the importance of writing down the event, story, illustration, or analogy as soon as you spot it. Otherwise, you will forget.

You will gather information from books, periodicals, and the Internet, but spend at least as much time drawing on your own knowledge and "interviewing" other people. To get input from other people, just ask. If you were preparing a speech on gender issues in communication, you could tell friends, neighbors, relatives, and colleagues that you were working on a presentation on communication between men and women, and that you would like to ask them a few questions to get their input. If they agree, ask them questions like: "What is your biggest frustration in communicating with the opposite sex? What topics are most difficult? Easiest? Is it more difficult to communicate with someone you know or with someone you have just met? Why? Is there a difference between communicating with the opposite gender at work compared to elsewhere? What's different? What are some examples? What do you see as the differences in the ways men communicate with women compared to communicating with other men? What do you see as the differences in the ways women communicate with men compared to communicating with other women?" Ask several people these kinds of questions, and you will soon have stories and illustrations and new points for your speech that you likely would not have come up with on your own.

Depending on your topic, you could do a simple survey and keep track of the results. Compare how men and women answer the question, for example. Or you could give people a brief written survey. Limit it to a maximum of 10 questions.

After you have gathered material from your reading, your "interviews," and your own experience and observations, you are ready for the next step in organizing your presentation.

❏ STEP 3: Arrange

Many speeches are hard to follow or remember because they do not have a clear structure or pattern. Too often, speakers amble through their material as sheep or goats would roam through a pasture, nibbling at this tuft of an idea and then moving on, without telling you, to totally different points that catch their attention. Unfortunately, neither these speakers nor what they are saying keep their audiences' attention.

Giving a presentation or speech is like leading a walking tour of a busy city that your audience has never visited. The members of your audience, like those of a tour group, do not know where you are going. They may not be easily led and may be easily distracted. If you start walking without orienting them, they may soon become lost. If they get distracted, they may not notice that you have changed directions unless you announce clearly where you were going. If you do not have an itinerary or a plan, they may not be able to rejoin you if they get lost.

For communication to be clear, effective, and easy to follow, it must be organized. An effective business letter opens with an introduction of the topic and why the person is writing (beginning), states and elaborates on the main point or points (middle), suggests what further action is expected, and signs off (ending). At a minimum, your presentation should have a clear beginning, middle, and end because this structure helps people follow and stay with you.

The classic design for a beginning, middle, and end for a speech is: "Tell them what you are going to tell them (beginning). Tell them (middle). Tell them what you told them (ending)." This is a useful overall approach for most presentations.

How to Begin Your Presentation

What do you want to accomplish in the first couple minutes of your presentation? I suggest that you want to:

- Get your audience's attention.
- Answer the unspoken questions they have of what they will get out of the presentation: "What's in it for them?" and "Why should they listen to you?" Give them reasons for wanting to hear what you are going to say.
- Orient them to what you will be talking about so they will know what to listen for.

Getting Your Audience's Attention

Do not assume you already will have the audience's attention just because they have come to hear a presentation on your subject. Most people's attention is scattered and unfocused when a speaker stands up to speak. They may be thinking about other members of the audience, a conversation they just finished, who you remind them of, how warm it is, why their friend sounded curt on the phone, whether this topic will be interesting, whether they will get answers to their questions, what they are missing by being at this meeting, and much more. Your beginning needs to grab their interest and focus their attention with enough drawing power that they will stop thinking about all the other things on their minds and they will listen and keep listening to what you are saying.

What are the best ways to begin a speech and get people's attention? No one way is the best way, and you may use different beginnings for the same speech, with different audiences. Here are fifteen effective ways to begin a speech with an example of each approach.

1. Tell a personal story or anecdote. Example: (This example could begin a speech on dealing with death and grief.) "I remember the first time I saw a person who was dead. I was probably 8 years old when my parents took me with them to a funeral home on the way home from church. I didn't know the elderly woman lying in the casket, but I did know that she looked very different from anyone I had ever seen. I was curious about what her skin would feel like, and I was also a little scared. But I was not sad. I felt no tears. My first experience with deep grief came about 5 years later when my grandma died."

2. Use a quotation as a point of takeoff. Example: "We are what we repeatedly do," according to Aristotle. If that's true, who are you? Who am I?"

3. Ask a rhetorical question. Example: "Can talking about something actually change it?"

4.   State a fact or statistic. Example: "We spend the equivalent of a year of our lives waiting in lines."

5.   Start with an intriguing prop and draw analogies or connections. Example: "How many uses can you think of in one minute for this pencil? Most of the time we only think of one. And yet our minds are capable of almost infinite innovation if we step out of the narrow limits we habitually draw around the problems we try to solve."

6.   Start with an historic event. Example: "On this day 85 years ago, Sigmund Freud published a book that would change forever how we think about human behavior."

7.   State your title and then jump in from there. Example: "'Dealing With Difficult People.' Every time I mention the topic to people, without exception, someone says: I need to know how to do that better!"

8.   Compliment your audience. Example: "I've been looking forward to meeting with you ever since I was invited. You have a reputation for excellent care that is known throughout the region."

9.   Show that you know something about them. Example: "I wasn't even alive when the ARC was founded. And for more years than I can remember, you've been helping parents deal with the trials, the needs, and the special experience of parenting an exceptional child."

10. Refer to the occasion. Example: "We are here because this is National Mental Health Month. But more than that, we're here because each of us has been touched in some way by the challenge of mental illness."

11. Tell them you've been looking forward to this talk and why. Example: "I've been looking forward to meeting with you because my first teacher changed my life. I know that a teacher's job is often a thankless one. But I'm here to tell you that you touch people in so many ways you never know about. And I'm here to thank you on behalf of so many children who are better off because of you and your dedication."

12. Say something provocative. Example: "Why is it that when a man cries, we think there's something wrong with him? The truth is that crying is normal and healthy. Always holding in the tears is what's abnormal."

13. Ask a question. Example: "How many of you can remember what you were doing when you learned that Kennedy had been shot? How many of you remember what color outfit your spouse, partner, or boss was wearing yesterday?"

14. Refer to a recent headline or news story. Example: "According to a recent poll reported in *The Wall Street Journal*, the most important single factor in job satisfaction for people with children was whether they felt their supervisors and employers supported them in making their family a high priority."

15. Create a scenario. Example: "Imagine this. Tomorrow you're sitting at your desk and you get a call telling you that you've won a $5 million lottery—$250,000 per year for 20 years. You didn't buy the ticket, but a favorite aunt bought the ticket in your name and she wants you to have it all." (This could lead into a speech on values, change, or life purpose, for example.)

Why Should Anyone Listen and What Should They Listen For?

Getting an audience's attention is not as difficult as keeping their interest. To keep their attention, you must answer their questions of why they should listen to you and what they will get out of the presentation. You also must give them an idea of what's coming and what to listen for.

A good formula for opening any presentation is this:

1. Get the audience's attention.
2. Tell them what you will be talking about and relate it to their world and to the benefits they will get from your talk.
3. Tell them something about yourself that will make them want to hear what you have to say about the topic.

To get your audience's attention, no matter what other technique you use to begin your speech, relate your topic immediately to something that directly affects the audience members and their world.

Consider a typical way that speakers begin informal educational presentations: "My topic tonight is panic attacks. I want to begin by talking about panic attacks, what they are and what they feel like, and some of the various forms they can take. Then I want to tell you about the treatments that have been most effective, because there is hope for people suffering from panic attacks. And I want to end by talking about how friends and family can be most helpful to someone with panic attacks. After that, I'll open the floor to questions and we'll take all the questions we have time for." This simple introduction might be enough to get and hold the attention of people who were already interested in panic attacks, either because of their own experience or that of someone they know. At least it tells people what they will learn and what to expect.

Now consider the following beginning for a presentation on the same topic: "Chances are at least 80% that either you or someone you know has had a panic attack. The intense episodes of anxiety that we call panic attacks may send more people to the emergency room than actual heart attacks. If you don't think you know anyone who has had a panic attack, it may be because people often keep quiet about them because they're afraid other people won't understand. Tonight I want to explain what panic attacks are, how they feel, how to recognize one, what we know about causes, how they can be treated (and they are highly treatable), and how you can help if someone you know suffers from panic attacks. I know you'll have questions and I'll make sure we have time for questions at the end."

Do you see the difference between the two beginnings? The first approach puts all the emphasis on the topic itself and what will be covered. The second approach gives as much information about the topic, but relates the topic immediately to the audience members' world and why they would benefit from listening. The first speaker may later make some of the same points about how common panic attacks are.

But by then many members of the audience may have lost interest because they did not see the relevance for themselves.

To make the beginning even more powerful, answer the question, without boasting or bragging, of why they should listen to you or why you are qualified to speak on this subject. In the "panic attack" example, you might go on to say: "As a therapist, I have treated dozens of clients suffering from panic disorder, many of whom were very demoralized by how it was limiting their lives. Without exception, these clients are enjoying fuller lives with full or significant improvement from their panic symptoms. This is not because I am so great but because the treatments we have today are so effective that no one needs to suffer the way they did even a few years ago from undiagnosed and untreated panic disorder."

How to Organize the Middle of Your Presentation

Once you have told people what you are *going* to tell them, you *tell* them. This is the main part or content of your presentation. This is also the longest part. For your sake and the audience's, you need to find a way to organize how you present your material.

Imagine your points, subpoints, stories, and illustrations as a set of photographic slides or snapshots lying in a jumbled heap on your desk. The pile of photographs is an analogy for the various "pieces" you may want to include in your presentation. In our analogy, the "pictures" are images collected from many places and times, perhaps from many vacations and family gatherings as well as landscapes and cityscapes you have taken. Your task is to organize them into a cohesive and organized "story." Although you could start picking them up one at a time, commenting on slides in no particular order, you could develop a more effective presentation, if you spent time sorting and arranging the pictures in an order that made sense, that fit together, that told a story. You would also improve the presentation if you eliminated photos that were similar or duplicates, and choose the best photos to illustrate the points you want to make. To organize them, however, you would need to know your topic and your main point. "My photographs" is too broad and has no point, as are "My Travels" and "My Family." Suppose you decide to do a presentation on "How Travel Changes One's View of the World." You would choose and arrange the photographs in a way to explain and illustrate your main points and subpoints.

In most presentations, the speaker is arranging words (and perhaps word pictures), stories, examples, and explanations to make points. What follows is a list of 16 different ways to organize the "pieces of content" of a speech. Some of the ways overlap with one another, as you will see, but I have included this long list to make it easier for you to find ways to organize your material. I suggest examples of how each one could be used as the organizational pattern for a presentation on communication or another topic.

1. Organize by who, what, where, when, why, and how. Example 1: A presentation on communication mistakes at work and how to avoid them could list examples of what people do (who and what), what the circumstances are (when and where), why they tend to make these mistakes, and how they could avoid or recover from the mistakes. Example 2: A presentation on panic disorder might be divided into what it is, who it affects, when and where it shows up, what causes it (why), and how people with panic disorder, including their friends and family, can deal with it.

2. Organize by topics, perhaps using alliteration for your key points. Example 1: Three points of a speech on honesty in relationships could be based on the words *caring, communication, courage.* Example 2: A speech on creating balance might focus on work, self, relationships, and spirit.

3. Describe a problem and solution(s). This pattern may include a call to action. Example: Problem of conflict avoidance. Solutions might be examining one's fears and attitudes about conflict; learning low threat strategies for dealing with conflict; developing support for dealing with conflict.

4. Present your subject from the viewpoint of chronological order (first, next, last). Example 1: Steps in communication process: listen, clarify, empathize, respond. Example 2: A speech on the stages of grief or the phases of adult development.

5. Present your subject in terms of past, present, and future (or any two of these). Example 1: Communication patterns between teens and their parents in the generation we grew up, in the present generation, and what trends may be developing for the future. Example 2: Psychotropic medication in the past; current medications; medications being tested for future release.

6. Describe your topic in experiential order. This is a variation of chronological order but may be especially appropriate for some coaches' and therapists' presentations. Example: How talking can change things: my past attitude and perspective; my experience causing me to reexamine the evidence, my new point of view.

7. Organize by priorities (most important, next most important, third most important, or vice versa). Example 1: Three communication patterns women wish men would do differently: least important—ask for directions; more important—listen without giving advice; most important—talk more about what they are feeling. Example 2: Three things children need most, starting with the most important.

8. Describe a situation's cause and effect. (Here is what happened and here is the result.) Example 1: Common customer communication mistakes and what the effects are. Example 2: The events of 9/11 and the way they have affected our worldview.

9. Organize the points by spatial or geographical order or proximity (local, regional, national, global). Examples: Overcoming we–they attitudes in our communication: looking at how it could happen at local, regional, national, and global levels. Example 2: Ways to market one's services: local, regional, national, global.

10. Present a model or theory and then discuss the evidence or the implications, or start with specific facts or observations and

draw conclusions from them (the first is called deductive reasoning and the latter is called inductive reasoning). Example: Virginia Satir's model of communication and the implications for the audience.

11. Present the material based on the scientific method (background and purpose, materials and methodology, results, recommendations). Example: Describe a communication survey or research project and the results.

12. Compare and contrast or present the pros and cons, strengths and weaknesses, or SWOT (strengths, weaknesses, opportunities, and threats). Example: Pros and cons of a command and direct style of management vs. a collaborative style of management.

13. Provide theory and reality. Another variation is myths and the truth/reality. Example 1: Three myths about communication: We usually think we are good communicators; we usually think communication should be easy; we usually think the other person is the problem. Example 2: "We believe we care about children in this country, but the reality is that our children our poorer, more malnourished, and less likely to live to adulthood than in any other industrialized nation."

14. Tell a story and draw lessons or conclusions from it. Example: A story of how a child responded to 9/11 could lead to points on how to protect our children, how to talk with our children about scary things, and how our children can also teach and help us.

15. Use an analogy or metaphor and draw lessons or conclusions from it. Example: In a speech on grudges, you might say that holding grudges is like drinking poison because you feel like killing somebody. Conclusions: You want to punish the person for what they did, but you are not really hurting them. The person you are really hurting is yourself. You can work through your anger in more productive ways.

16. Use a phrase, quote, or word and break it into parts or draw your points from it. Example: *Communicate* comes from two words: "ko" and "mei," which mean "to work" and "together."

Develop your points around what the "work" of communication and is how communication is something we do "together."

You may use more than one organizational pattern at the same time. For example, a listing of points may also be arranged in sequential order. A presentation on dealing with difficult people might include a step-by-step process: ask, listen, empathize, clarify.

As you are deciding about your main points and gathering information and stories, experiment with different ways of organizing your presentation. A presentation on learning to listen to children could be organized as a "how to" with a series of steps. The same speech could be organized as "problem and solutions," with the first part of the speech describing problem behaviors in children that then are shown to be helped by sensitive and patient listening (solution). In this example, the "problem and solutions" approach would probably be more engaging and interesting for the audience. Developing and describing the "pain" of the problem before presenting solutions is more engaging than simply giving a list of techniques for listening.

One way to think about the best order for what you say in a presentation is to ask yourself, "What is the first thing a person needs to know to understand this topic?" For informational presentations, often the first thing people need to know is "What do you mean by _____?" (whatever your presentation is about). They may need to know what *you* mean by the term you are using. If you use a term like *depression* or *anxiety* or *substance abuse*, even with an audience of therapists, you may need to clarify what aspects you are talking about so you are all "on the same page." If as a coach, you use the term *balance* with a group of accountants, they may be thinking of balancing an accounting ledger. Clarify what you are talking about. Plan or revise your presentation by asking again and again, "What is the next thing my audience needs to know or understand about this topic?"

How can you decide which organization is best for your presentation? Here are a few suggestions:

- Consider the audience's knowledge and experience with the topic. If they know little about the topic, organize your presentation from the simplest to the most complex, or use a basic sequential order. Past, present, and future is also easy to follow.
- Consider the audience's overall personality style. If you know you are speaking to scientists, academics, engineers, physicians, or others who tend to emphasize logic and analytical thinking, emphasize the logic in your organization. Use cause and effect, scientific method, problem and solution, or theory and reality approach, for example. If you know your audience is likely to be more intuitive and oriented to feelings, use a metaphor or tell a story as the basis of your key points.
- If in doubt, use a simple organizational structure. You can develop the complexity and subtlety in your ideas, but keep the organization as clear and simple as possible.
- Most of all, choose an organization that works for you—one that flows well and is easy for you to remember. If you like and are comfortable with the structure of your talk, and it is simple and clear, it will probably work for your audience too.

Organizing Each Point of Your Presentation

As you decide on an overall way to organize your presentation, you will be faced with how to organize each of your subpoints as well. Even if you have a clear overall structure, if your individual points are not organized, your audience will still find your presentation hard to follow. A useful pattern for *each* subpoint is:

1. Introduction
2. Your point stated in one sentence
3. Explanation and examples
4. Stories and anecdotes, facts and statistics, quotations, and restatements
5. Summary statement
6. Transition to next point or conclusion

The introduction to each point in your presentation prepares your audience to listen, gets their attention again, and leads them into this section of your presentation. In a presentation on how women and men can better understand one another, an introduction to a point might be: "Men and women often make fun of the idiosyncrasies of the other when it comes to communication. Part of our culture has been to joke about women gossiping and men never asking for directions. But beyond the joking and the 'battle of the sexes' is also something to be valued and affirmed about the truth that we conceal with our stereotypes."

Make it easy for your audience to follow the "tour" of your presentation by summarizing regularly and giving them clear signals when you change directions. In a presentation, the changes of direction from one point to another are called transitions. Transitions are like road signs on the highway that help us know we will be making a turn. Use a transition *every time* you move to a new point to help the audience make the turn with you. The basic formula for a transition is to summarize or recap what you have just said in the previous point and tell the audience that you are now moving to another point. You are saying, in effect, "This is what we have just been talking about. *Now*, we're going to talk about this *next* thing." For example: "I've described the problem. Now I want to tell you about some possible solutions." Or, "We've talked about ways to create 'breathing space' at work. Let's look next at ways to make space for yourself at home." Or, "The first two steps, as we've seen, are taking time to listen to our children, and drawing them out by asking open-ended questions. But the third step may be the most challenging and underused of all: responding to our children with empathy instead of giving them advice."

How to End Your Presentation

An important transition is the conclusion or ending of your presentation. The importance of endings is often overlooked even though the last thing said can be the main thing someone remembers. If you end your speech awkwardly or drag out your conclusion, you may lose the positive connection you had made earlier with your audience.

What are the keys to a good ending?

Come to a clear, decisive, and "on-time" ending. Children are not the only ones who want to know, "Are we there yet?" Audiences can get very frustrated by speakers who run over their allotted time. Unless a speaker is exceptionally dynamic, the audience may stop listening and start thinking, "I wish he would shut up!" Instead, by ending on time or a few minutes early, you may leave members of your audience thinking to themselves, "I really enjoyed that presentation. I wish I could hear more."

Do not simply drift off or wind down like a battery that has run out of juice. An audience will not leave inspired or energized by a speaker who ends the presentation by shuffling notes and saying, "Well, I guess that's all I have to say."

Plan your closing in advance. The four most common and effective endings are a summary, a thank you, a story, and a challenge. Whichever ending you choose, make it quick and energetic. One of the most effective closings ties the ending to where you began, as in this example: "Does treatment work? Remember Robert, the boy I told you about in the beginning? He graduated from college last year and will be starting medical school in the fall. He almost became a human casualty because his learning problems were misdiagnosed. Instead, he can now become a healer and a helper."

If possible, plan an alternative ending that is brief and bare bones in case you need to cut your speech short. Instead of summarizing all your points, you might close with a challenge such as: "You've heard about the challenge. You understand the issues better than before. What really matters is what you do with what you've learned. I hope you will decide to act and act now. That's the only thing that will change any of this." We will discuss more ways to shorten your speech in the next chapter.

Consider saving your real closing until after the question-and-answer period. Since question-and-answer periods are unpredictable and may not end on a strong note, save an ending for after the last question. You can lead into the question-and-answer period by saying something like, "I know I have probably raised questions for some of you, and before I make my final remarks, I'd like to give you a chance to ask your questions." Then, after the question-and-answer period, you can end with a summary, a thank you, or a challenge that will end your speech on a positive and memorable note.

To be effective and flexible with the ending, as well as the rest of the presentation, you will need to practice, the final step of preparation.

❏ STEP 4: Practice, Play, and Prune

Try giving the speech first to an empty room. Do this several times, until you are feeling reasonably familiar and comfortable with the content. After a couple of practice sessions, record yourself giving the speech. If possible, use a camcorder so you can see *and* hear yourself. If you do not have access to a camcorder, record yourself with a tape or digital recorder. Make notes while you listen. You will see and hear things on the tape that you want to change or improve. Listen and watch for those places where you jump from one subject to another without warning. Listen for places where you sense the speech does not work well or where you do not like the wording. Listen and watch for nervous gestures—"uh's" and "you know's," throat clearing, or other habitual ways you make a sound instead of simply pausing (these are called vocalized pauses). Practice making changes and then tape it again. If you do this two or three times, you will likely be pleasantly surprised at the improvements you will see.

Give the speech to one or two supportive friends or coaches. Ask them to tell you what they liked and remembered. Ask them where they had trouble hearing or following you or when they wanted you to go slower or faster. Try not to be defensive if they do not like or understand everything. They are giving you a gift in the form of honest, helpful feedback.

One goal of practicing is to make the presentation as clear and easy to understand as possible. Keep revising the organization as well as the examples and illustrations until the presentation flows smoothly and your "audience" stays with you from beginning to end. Another goal is to become completely familiar and comfortable with the presentation, so that you can move around instead of being frozen to the podium. The more familiar you are with what you will say, the less nervous you will be and the more you can focus on connecting with your audience. A third goal is to become familiar enough with the language you are using that you can emphasize the appropriate words and phrases for maximum impact while sounding natural and conversational.

This is also the time to prune anything that does not add to the impact. You will not know which parts drag or go on too long until you practice aloud.

This may sound like a lot of work for a simple speech. Think of a play that takes weeks of rehearsal or a concert that involves hours of practice. Your speech is a performance and requires the same kind of preparation and practice. If you are willing to put the effort into your presentation, you will be well rewarded.

WORKSHEET 5.1. Speech Preparation

Instructions: The questions in this worksheet are designed to generate ideas, structure, and approaches to preparing your speech. They will not write the speech for you, but they can trigger helpful ideas and ways of thinking. You will find these questions most helpful if you write out responses so that you tap into thoughts and ideas that are below the surface level of your awareness. Don't worry if you cannot complete many of the questions the first time. Fill in what you can and more ideas will come.

1.   What are your primary objectives in this speech? To inform, educate, inspire, challenge, entertain, persuade, etc.? Pick one or two *main* purposes.

2.   What is your presentation about? State your topic in one sentence. Try several versions until you get one you can work with. (If you are not sure about your topic, pick one topic and work on it. You can change the topic later, but it is very difficult to start developing a speech without a topic.)

3.   What points do you want to make? List several "points" or areas you would want to cover in your speech.

4.   What are the points that you feel are the strongest, the most important, the most interesting, or the most challenging? Underline them.

5.   How will you organize your main points? Look earlier in this chapter at the list of ways to organize a speech. Try arranging your main points using several of the organizational strategies listed there. Decide on the one that works best.

6.   What stories or anecdotes could you use to illustrate each of your points? (Consider personal and family stories, stories of clients, and classical stories from movies, literature, the Bible, and mythology.)

7.   What personal experience have you had with any point you want to make? Have you had any humorous or embarrassing

experiences that relate? (Obviously, you need to use good judgment in relating personal experiences.)

8. What examples and analogies could you use to support each of your points? See what comes to mind if you brainstorm several ways to complete the sentence: "_____" (your topic) is like _____. For example, "taking time for oneself" is like letting the rough waves calm down, like letting the sediment settle and water clear, like filling up a water pitcher before it is empty, like plugging the hole in the canoe instead of always having to bail out the water, like having reserve supplies in your larder.

9. Are there physical objects that symbolize your topic or some aspect of your topic? For example, in a presentation on what it means to care about a person, I might bring three tangible objects that convey acts of caring I experienced: a dish to symbolize food from a neighbor, a handwritten note from a friend, and a telephone to symbolize how even a phone call can make us feel cared about. I often get ideas for objects by wandering around my house, office, or yard looking for symbolic articles.

10. Are there famous or historical people or examples who illustrate what you are talking about? For example: CBS's Mike Wallace suffered from depression or NBC weathercaster Willard Scott dealt successfully with panic disorder.

11. What recent news events tie in to your topic?

12. What quotations can you find that fit with your topic? Use quotation books like Bartlett's as well as your own books. Many books begin each chapter with a good quote.

13. What are the human emotions underlying your topic? How can you help people in the audience identify with these emotions?

14. What do most people *not* know about your topic that you believe they need to know?

15. Are there statistics that illustrate the scope of the problem you are talking about? If so, how could you make the figures more memorable?

16. What are misconceptions or myths about your topic?
17. What assumptions about your topic need to be questioned?
18. What would you like to change about how the audience thinks about the topic?
19. What theories or paradigms apply to your topic? Is there one that would help your audience understand the topic better or in a new way? (Examples: Satir, Maslow, etc.)
20. What is there about your topic or one of your points that relates to someone overcoming a challenge? How has it brought out a hidden strength or quality? How has it forced someone to grow? How has it changed how someone, including you, looked at situations or people?
21. How does your topic affect relationships between people? How does it hurt, help, change, or heal relationships?
22. How have members of your audience probably experienced the topic or problem you are talking about? How can you evoke or include their experience in your speech?
23. What do you want your audience to take away from your speech? Do you have an idea of how you want to end the speech? Is there a story or quote or challenge that would make a strong ending? Is there a way to connect your ending to where you began the speech?
24. Think about your topic in relation to the *particular* audience to which you will be speaking. Answer any of the following questions that apply:

    a. Why are they there?
    b. What do they want from you?
    c. What is important to them?
    d. What problems do they have?
    e. What are they concerned about?
    f. What do they know about the subject?
    g. What do they want to know?
    h. What are their questions likely to be?

i. What is the best way to give them what they want?

j. What would make them glad they listened to your presentation?

k. What aspects of your subject will:

- Answer a problem faced by the audience?
- Pique the curiosity of your listeners?
- Support or challenge the beliefs of your audience?
- Add to the background your listeners need?
- Strike your listeners as new and unique?
- Recall pleasurable memories for your listeners?
- Increase listeners' respect for you?
- Relieve anxieties or doubts felt by your listeners?
- Give the group information they need for decision-making?
- Excite, inspire, or thrill your audience?

CHAPTER 6

Delivering an Effective Presentation

PUBLIC SPEAKING IS AN unnatural act where one person stands up and delivers a monologue of 15 to 60 minutes to a group of people the speaker does not know on a topic they have not discussed. The burden is on the speaker to make it work. It is no wonder that many people dread and avoid doing public speaking. If you want to give effective presentations, think of your presentations as informative, energetic conversations with people instead of public speaking.

Conversation is natural. We greet someone and they reply. We ask a question and they answer. They tell us what concerns them and we respond. In a conversation between two people, both are involved.

A presentation is a different kind of conversation, but it should be a conversation nevertheless. In a presentation that is a conversation instead of a monologue, the audience members feel that you are talking with them about something they are actively interested in. They are responding and reacting to what you are saying, inwardly if not out loud.

No matter what type of presentation you give, here are keys to doing it well (we will develop these points throughout this chapter):

- "Get set" to give a good presentation.

- Involve your audience from the beginning to the end of your presentation.
- Engage your whole self when you speak.
- Use your voice effectively.
- Use audiovisuals with purpose.
- Plan in advance for the unexpected.
- Know how you will end the presentation, including how to make it shorter if necessary.
- Allow time for a question-and-answer period at the end.

❏ "GETTING SET" TO GIVE A GOOD PRESENTATION

We discussed in the previous chapter how to prepare and practice your presentation. As the day of your presentation draws nearer, take measures to be at your best and avoid being rushed. Decide several days before what you will wear for the presentation. Arrange for any needed mending, laundering, or dry cleaning. Prepare any handouts and have them copied well in advance. Try to get a good sleep the night before so you will be well rested.

For the presentation itself, allow enough time to arrive early for the meeting so you can check out the room and mix with the audience, if possible. Check out where you will be speaking as early as possible to avoid last-minute problems. Make sure you know where you're speaking, how to use the microphone, and what happens before and after you speak. Talk with the person who will be introducing you and make sure that person has your introduction. By meeting a few people ahead of time, you will learn more about the audience and have a few friendly faces to draw support from as you start your speech.

Before you begin speaking, pause briefly, take a deep breath, and make eye contact. This can help you get centered and also give the audience time to pay attention. One of the most effective ways to engage the audience is to make eye contact with one person at a time, holding the contact through a phrase, thought, or sentence. This takes practice since many of us "scan" the audience and don't look at anyone for more than a second or two. As you learn to focus on one audience member at a time, your impact will improve dramatically.

Start your speech with some extra energy. If you are a very relaxed person, as many psychotherapists are, you may need to psych yourself up a little at the start.

Get off to a quick start. Do not spend time on lengthy thank you's and acknowledgments. Your audience will decide in the first few minutes whether you have something to say that will interest them, so you want to draw them in right away with a strong opening that relates to something they are interested in and that tells them what they will learn by listening.

❏ INVOLVING YOUR AUDIENCE THROUGHOUT

Think for a moment of speakers you found boring. Did they engage the audience? Did they ask the audience questions? Did they connect what they were saying to the audience's situation? Did they make good eye contact with the audience? Did they seem interested in the audience? Probably not.

Now think of speakers you found interesting and stimulating. How did they engage the audience? Did they ask questions? Did they ask the audience about their own experience? Did they relate their comments to the situation of audience members? Did they make eye contact and seem interested in the audience? Most likely they did.

You may think that what is most important in a presentation is what you say and how you say it. In fact, what is most important is whether the audience stays engaged and involved. If they don't, it doesn't really matter what you say. The audience will not hear it or remember it or be changed by it. If the audience members do get engaged, they will take what you say and apply it to themselves and their situations. They will ask questions and find out what they want to know. And they will think you are an excellent speaker because you spoke in a way that interested them.

Fortunately, involving your audience involves skills and techniques you can learn. It is easy to do, in part because most audiences want to be involved.

What are good ways to keep your audience involved and reacting to what you say?

Ask Questions

One of the best ways to involve your audience and get a reading on where they are is to ask questions. For a presentation on parenting, a therapist might ask, "What's the hardest thing for you to handle as a parent?" or "If you could do one thing better as a parent, what would it be?" A coach might ask: "What's something you love to do that you haven't done in at least three months? How is your life different when you take the time for this activity?" In these examples, you might let several people give short answers to the question. Within 2 or 3 minutes, you have not only engaged the audience, but also have gathered examples that you know will resonate with several members of the audience. You can then incorporate these responses and your knowledge of the audience's interests into the rest of your talk.

You can be like a ventriloquist with people's unspoken questions, such as "You may be thinking: This doesn't apply to me. But every single person here knows someone who. . . ."

You can get people involved by asking them to remember something or picture something or do something. For example: "Remember how much simpler life was when you were growing up? We played in the neighborhood every summer evening until dark and nobody thought to worry. Nobody *needed* to worry."

You can use questions to ask for experiences or examples, as above. You can also use them to get a show of hands, one- or two-word answers, or simply an inner acknowledgment or nod of the head from the audience as a whole.

Here are some examples:

Show of hands: "How many of you are willing to admit you don't get enough sleep most nights?" "How many of you know someone who drinks too much?" "How many of you have taken a class just for fun during the past year?" "If you were given the choice between making more money or having more time off, how many would choose more money? How many would choose more time off?"

One- or two-word answers: "What one or two words come to mind when you hear the word *depression*?" "I'd like you to shout out one word that describes something you are afraid of." "Does anybody know how much time the average couple spends talking with each other during an average week? What would you guess?"

Inner acknowledgment or nod of head: "Have you ever felt like you would go over the edge if somebody asked you to do one more thing?" "Do you ever dream of living on an island where you never had to deal with another person ever again?" Rhetorical questions can stimulate thinking instead of soliciting an answer.

To get the most out of asking questions, respond to the answers. At least acknowledge them with a yes or an uh-huh or a thank you. If you ask for a sharing of examples or experiences, respond with empathy or appreciation if possible. For example, to the parent who says that the hardest thing they have to handle as a parent is dealing with their children's fighting, you might say, "It's often hard to know what's best to do, isn't it?" To people who say that they feel bigger and more at peace when they take the time to paint, you might say "It's amazing what a difference a creative activity can make in how we feel, isn't it?" Try to remain positive and open-minded even if someone says something with which you disagree. Now is not the time to debate issues or hammer out differences with audience members.

If you have asked the question as a lead-in to a point you want to make, make the connection quickly and clearly. If you give a presentation on how to get a good night's sleep and begin with one or more questions asking how many don't get enough sleep and how many have trouble falling asleep after a busy day, then move directly into your core message. For example: "Getting a good night's sleep is not easy for many of us in a culture that encourages doing more and more. And even though there are not always simple answers for improving our sleep, I will teach you some of the best methods for improving sleep based on the latest sleep research."

If you ask questions as a way to involve your audience, don't let their responses sidetrack your presentation. If someone asks you a question in response to your question, you may choose not to answer it, saying, "That's a good question and I'll be talking about that later in my presentation," or "That's a great question but unfortunately a little more involved than we have time for tonight. If you'll check back with me afterward, I'll be glad to suggest some resources."

If someone goes on too long in answer to a question, you may need to interrupt and say something like: "Thank you. In order to cover everything, I'm going to keep moving, but you've given us a good example" or "I can see that this is really important to you" or something similar that fits.

Remember that the audience is counting on you to be in charge. You are the only one who knows what you want to cover and who can keep things moving. Ask questions, but do not abdicate control.

Relate What You Are Saying to Specific Members of the Audience or to Something About the Community, Organization, or Occasion

Learning about an organization ahead of time enables you to weave in facts or stories you have learned about them. It is an effective way to customize your presentation and involve your audience at the same time.

If you are able to meet and talk with audience members ahead of time, either by phone or as the meeting begins, you will be able to allude to one or more members by name. "Jim was telling me before the meeting about some of the incredible contributions you have made as an organization." Or "Sarah was telling me about an interesting example of this that she experienced." If you want to use someone's story as an example in your speech, make sure in advance that the person is comfortable with it, and ask if you may use the story in your presentation.

Even if you have not spoken to audience members in advance, find a way to relate your topic to the audience members' experience. For example, if you are speaking to a group of teachers about communication, you might say: "As teachers, you know better than most the importance of adjusting your communication style to your audience. You probably don't talk to students in exactly the same way you would talk to their parents, do you? By learning certain principles, you can be even more effective in doing what you now do without having to think about it." If you are talking to other professionals, therapists, or coaches about self-care, you might say: "I realize that every one of you is an expert in self-care. You help your clients identify what they need and give them permission to ease up on their unrealistically high standards. But we all know that it is easier to teach others how to take care of themselves than to do it for ourselves. So let's be honest about this. It doesn't come easy for many of us, including me. But the benefits we get when we stop ignoring our own needs make it worth the work and discomfort of getting there."

Ask the Audience to Do Something

You can ask people to stand up, move around, sing a song, find someone with a characteristic, pair up and talk about a topic you assign, do a stress reduction exercise, and so on. In workshops, you will likely include several activities. In presentations, make sure:

- You have a good reason for the activity.
- The audience will understand the purpose by the end of the activity.
- The activity will not create more disruption than it is worth (remember, you will have to get their attention again after the activity is over).
- You think through and practice the instructions in advance. Getting a group of people to do something they aren't expecting is usually harder than we realize and needs clear, well-paced

instructions. If possible, practice the exercise with friends or colleagues before using it publicly.

- The exercise is appropriately timed to your presentation length (e.g., don't do a 20-minute exercise in a 45-minute talk).

Use an Object as a Prop

A prop, like a picture, can be worth a thousand words if it conveys the message you want. I remember a speaker who started a speech by holding up an egg carton and asking what it was. Several people answered, "A dozen eggs," and when he opened it, there was a banana inside. Then he held up a tomato juice can and asked what it was. One or two brave souls said it was a can of tomato juice and he reached in and pulled out an egg. He then held up a book and a few people said it was a book, but the speaker had carved out the inside and hidden a bell in it. "How often do you jump to conclusions about what something is, or *who* someone is, based on what they look like they would be?" he asked. The speaker had engaged everyone in the audience and made a point that we would not easily forget, all within 2 minutes of beginning his presentation.

Another speaker used two potted plants, a cactus, and a fern, asking the audience what growing conditions each needed. Then he asked the audience what would happen if he gave the cactus lots of water and kept the fern in a hot dry area. The audience answered that the plants would probably not survive. They certainly wouldn't thrive. The speaker used the illustration as the launching of a presentation on the importance of understanding and responding to the unique needs of different people.

Beware of using a prop that is too trite or obvious. The audience must not be able to see your point before you make it. Unless the prop enables an element of suspense or not knowing, the audience will not be engaged. Also, do not overuse props. I saw a speaker begin his presentation with a chest from which he extracted objects, one after another, making a point with each one. By the fifth or sixth object, the entire audience was hoping that there were no more objects to be extracted. Instead of engaging his audience, he lost us by overdoing it.

Respond to the Audience's Nonverbal Signals

If you pay attention to your audience, you will be aware of signals that they are not fully involved. People begin to shift restlessly, look around or check their watches, or engage in side conversations. With experience and practice, you will be able to notice these signs and take action quickly. The action needed depends on why you are losing them. Have you gone past the allotted time? If so, bring your presentation to a close quickly. Have you let your own energy drop and started speaking in a monotone? If so, move around more, consciously increase your vocal variety, or speak louder. Are you belaboring a point without examples or stories? If so, give an illustration or ask the audience for examples of what you are talking about.

If you don't know why you are losing people, you can comment on what you are observing: "I'm seeing quite a few eyes glazing over and sense that I'm missing somewhere with you. What about this is not making sense or connecting for you?" Or " I get the sense that some of you disagree with what I'm saying. Am I right, and would you be willing to tell me what you disagree with?"

It takes courage to invite people to tell you what's going on, but the alternative is that you lose them anyway. You may find that you are misreading their nonverbal signals. You may find that they are feeling challenged and uncomfortable by what you are saying, but they think you are absolutely right. Audiences will respect you for asking them what's going on, and you will probably win them back by doing so. The key is not to get defensive or take it personally. Approach it as a problem-solving exercise: You are trying to keep people involved, but it appears that you are not. You want to find out what you can do to get people engaged again.

Involve Your Audience Early and Keep Them Involved to the End

To involve your audience, you have to start early in the presentation and keep them involved to the end. One common mistake is not to engage the audience until the speaker senses that the audience is getting bored or restless. Then the speaker tries techniques to involve the audience, with no success. If you speak for several minutes before asking the audience a question, they will settle into the role of being passive listeners. Getting passive listeners involved after 10 minutes or more of monologue is almost as difficult as waking people out of a sound sleep and expecting them to engage immediately in conversation.

Another common mistake is starting out involving the audience with questions and personal references, and then lapsing into a monologue after the first few minutes. Audiences will feel alienated by this approach, as if the speaker is not really interested in what they have to say. Audiences need to be continually and regularly involved to stay interested, not just invited at the beginning of the talk and then ignored.

❑ ENGAGING YOUR WHOLE SELF WHEN YOU SPEAK

You will be most effective as a speaker if you are able to be yourself and use your whole body in your presentation. Many speakers, especially when they are nervous, report feeling they are playing a role, pretending they know what they are doing, but thinking only of the words and thoughts to say as they try to ignore the panicky fears of failure. They become "talking heads," unaware of much besides their thoughts, their voices, and perhaps their shaking knees or the butterflies in their stomachs. The role is an unconscious attempt to protect themselves from the perceived threat. As people discover that the threat they feel is exaggerated or even imagined, they realize they can be themselves.

Instead of engaging in this kind of role playing, make it your goal to be yourself with the group. This does not mean that you necessarily tell them everything you are thinking and feeling, such as how nervous you may be, but it does mean that you should be with the audience as you would be if you were telling a story or leading a conversation with a group of good friends. You do not need to put up a front or play a role. You connect to and speak from your authentic self.

Being yourself in front of a group does not come easily for many people. You may need to pay attention to how you feel when you are yourself. Many people say that when they are most themselves, they feel a centered, peaceful, warm, or alive feeling somewhere in the center of their body, somewhere between their lower abdomen and their heart area.

Lee Glickstein, the creator of Speaking Circles, describes this coming back into oneself, whether alone or in the presence of another person, as "being with." When we are able to "be with" ourselves and another person, we need not *do* anything. We need not perform. We can simply be who we are. He suggests practicing at least 2 minutes each day, starting by simply "being with" an object such as a rock or a piece of pottery. Next, seek out a safe and accepting partner to "be with" in silence for just 30 seconds in the beginning, letting your eyes meet while experiencing whatever you feel. Let your only goal be to be yourself while you sit with the other person. At first it will probably be awkward and uncomfortable, but with experience you will be able to be with the other person easily and naturally.

To learn to be yourself in front of a group, practice being yourself in small groups when you are simply a participant. Notice when you are playing a role or tuning out, and make a conscious practice of letting go of the role and coming back into yourself. Practice coming into yourself when you are practicing your presentation on your own. Then notice whether you move into a role when you practice in front of a group. If so, experiment with giving up the role and coming back into yourself.

Using your whole body as you speak can also improve your presentations and make you feel more confident and free. As I have suggested, many speakers shrink their awareness to tune out everything but their heads and throats. Here are ways to practice being aware of and moving your whole body when you speak.

1. Shift your weight forward on your feet and feel yourself stand a little straighter. Take a breath down into your belly and feel your diaphragm pushing the air up through your body.
2. When practicing, take two steps on a diagonal toward your imagined audience. Stop walking, plant your feet with one slightly more forward than the other, and make a point. Then pause, take a few steps in another direction, and plant your feet

again before continuing to speak. Imagine with your body as well as your mind that the sound of your voice is coming up through the soles of your feet, through your body, and out through your mouth. The purpose of this exercise is to develop a strong bodily sense of your voice as well as to practice pausing while you move from one point to another.

3. Notice whether you are holding your head and neck stiffly. If so, practice moving your head around as you speak, turning from side to side and tilting your head into different positions, as though expressing surprise, puzzlement, questioning, stubbornness, curiosity, and so forth. Move your head into different positions as though you were imitating a bird. It may sound silly, but if you practice moving your head freely while you speak, your speaking will become livelier and more interesting.

4. Now notice whether you are holding your elbows close to your body. Let them swing out naturally away from your body, almost like you are a bird flapping your wings gently. If you prefer, imagine that you are a choral director conducting a slow, flowing piece of music, moving your hands in the range between your hips and shoulders. The point of this exercise is to experience how much better it feels (and looks) when you let your arms move naturally instead of clenching them tightly against your body.

❏ USING YOUR VOICE EFFECTIVELY

Using your whole self when you speak includes using your voice effectively. You do not need a great actor's voice to be an effective public speaker, but you need to use your voice effectively in order to be heard and not to distract the audience by negative vocal patterns. Common problems that can interfere with your being heard are:

1. Not caring properly for your voice instead of developing good voice habits or avoiding vocal abuse, or both.

2.   Not speaking loudly enough for everything you say to be heard, including trailing off at the end of sentences.

3.   Not using enough variety in your voice (this is more often a problem for men).

4.   Using too many vocalized pauses (too many uh's or um's when you pause).

Here are ways to deal with these problems.

How to Take Care of Your Voice

Most of us take our voices for granted unless we develop laryngitis and cannot talk except to whisper. Public speaking puts demands on our voices quite different than everyday talking and can strain our voices, just as prolonged exercise can be a strain if you are unaccustomed to it.

Bonnie Raphael, a professional voice coach and head of the Professional Actor Training Program at the University of North Carolina, recommends that speakers regularly exercise their voices so that their voices will be strong, flexible, and responsive when they present. She suggests the following exercises (personal correspondence January 18, 2004):

- Do full-body yawns or stretches, allowing both the body and the voice to open up.
- Gently shake different areas of the body, such as hands, feet, arms, legs, and shoulders.
- Breathe out fully and then soften the belly, letting your body naturally inhale low into the torso. Exhale easily and fully without postural collapse. Repeat slowly about 6 times.
- Intertwine the fingers of both hands on the back of your skull. Without tensing your shoulders or holding your breath, pull forward with the elbows and back with the head steadily for about 20 to 30 seconds. Release, enjoying the new freedom and energy you feel in the back of your neck.
- With your hands on your shoulders, move your elbows forward and back to touch in front and approach each other in back,

repeating until the muscles fatigue slightly. With your hands on your shoulders, "flap your wings" slowly until the muscles fatigue slightly. With your hands on your shoulders, move your elbows in large circles, first forward and then backward until the muscles fatigue slightly. Raise and drop your shoulders until slightly fatigued.

- While facing straight forward, do slow head rolls first in one direction and then in the other, repeating a few times. Be sure to continue breathing throughout. If you have any neck problems or discomfort, half head rolls (from ear to chin to other ear and back to chin) are preferable.

- Use your tongue to explore all parts of your mouth as a way of loosening your tongue. With a relaxed jaw, move just your tongue from top lip to bottom lip to top lip to bottom lip as you say or sing, la-la-la-la-la-la-laaaahhh.

- Move the different parts of your face around slowly, taking care to continue to breath easily. Repeat more quickly until your facial muscles are slightly fatigued.

- Drop your jaw, take a breath, and release with a long vocalized sigh, starting high and finishing in the lower range. Avoid screeching on the high pitches or growling on the low ones. Do this 3 or 4 times.

- Use your fingers to gently rub and stimulate your face. With your hands gently covering the cheeks and eyes and the lips gently together, hum directly into the palms of your hands, feeling and enjoying the vibrations produced by your voice. Allow the pitches to move up and down while continuing to rub your face and hum. Then drop your hands and feel the vibrations in the bones of your face and skull as you continue humming.

- Say various combinations of tongue twisters with exaggerated articulation. For example: "Peter Piper picked a peck of pickled peppers." "Twelve twins twirled twelve twigs." "Fat frogs flying past fast." "Red lorry, yellow lorry, red lorry, yellow lorry." Before doing a particular presentation, memorize the first and last sentences of your speech and practice them immediately after these tongue twisters.

Here are some simple tips for caring for your voice:

- Do not smoke and avoid secondary smoke if possible. Reduce or avoid caffeine drinks (coffee, tea, and cola) before a presentation because they tend to dry out the throat. Avoid eating heavily before a presentation, as this compromises the capacity for the diaphragm to move up and down. You may want to avoid dairy products before an important presentation because they tend to coat your throat. Avoid shouting or excessive clearing of your throat. Sip warm or room temperature water before you speak to increase vocal fold lubrication. Ice water may tighten the throat. If you have dry mouth while speaking, gently bite the tip of your tongue to increase saliva flow.
- Consciously relax your throat before speaking by simulating and holding a yawn. You can do this without actually opening your lips so you do not appear tired or bored. You can also bring your awareness to your throat and jaw, noticing any tightness or tension and consciously letting it go just as you would let go of tension in your hands or feet.
- Practice good breath-support techniques to reduce straining and tightening your throat. A good way to do this is to take a breath down into your abdomen and then gently tighten your abdomen to create a steady pressure upward with your breath. Imagine that you are about to blow up a beach ball or blow out a candle. Notice how you gently but firmly tighten your abdominal wall. You are actually pushing up with your diaphragm. Practice speaking while holding this gentle pressure in your abdomen. Singers often practice pushing their hands together in front of them to create the pressure. You can also practice talking while pushing with both hands against a wall. The goal is to provide steady upward pressure from your abdomen so that you do not try to force your breath or your sound from your throat.
- If you have significant problems with your voice that these methods do not solve, you might want to consult a speech therapist or a voice and speech coach (see Resources).

How to Increase Volume

Consciously open your mouth wide when you talk. Think of your mouth as a megaphone that you can make larger to let more sound out. Speak with breath support from the diaphragm. Take a full belly breath; feel yourself releasing your breath from low in your torso as you form words. Practice speaking this way on a regular basis.

Practice releasing your voice forward into the front of your mouth, to the teeth and lips. Then practice speaking as though your voice is actually making its sound 3 feet in front of you, then 10 feet in front of you, and then in the middle of the audience. Make sure that you are speaking to rather than at your audience members,

When you start your presentation, begin speaking first to someone near the back of the room instead of someone near the front of the room. Exaggerate your enunciation. Emphasize not only the consonants but the resonant sounds as well (vowels and *ng*'s).

Take particular care to keep your volume and articulation strong through the ends of sentences. Speakers often are thinking ahead to their next sentence and let the volume drop. Instead, pause at the end of sentences to let the audience take in your words and ideas.

How to Increase Variety

Think of your voice as a musical instrument. Practice adding variety in pitch (higher and lower), pace (faster and slower), volume (softer and louder), emphasis (key words more than others), and pausing (like the rests in music). Pay attention to variety while practicing talks. Record yourself and listen for the melody. Read a children's story out loud with as much expression as possible impersonating each character as you read. Incorporate some of that expression into your speaking.

How to Avoid Vocalized Pauses

Practice pausing and allowing silence rather than feeling that you have to fill each pause with sound. Become aware of others' vocalized pauses. Listen to recordings of your presentation for unnecessary vocalization. Ask someone to count how many times you say "uh" or whatever you tend to say. Keep taping and listening to your presentations until you overcome any tendency to use vocalized pauses.

❑ USING AUDIOVISUALS WITH PURPOSE

Television has changed audiences. People are accustomed to constantly changing, highly stimulating visual entertainment. Does that mean you have to put on a television show to keep people's attention? No, but it does mean that you must remember that it's harder to get and keep people's attention than in the past. Audiovisuals *may* be a way to add interest to a presentation.

Deciding Whether to Use Audiovisuals

The decision whether to use audiovisuals depends on whether they will increase the interest, impact, and clarity of your presentation. For a workshop, audiovisuals may be essential. But for speeches to community and professional groups, audiovisuals can detract from people getting a sense of you as a person. Remember, *you* may be the best "audiovisual" for your presentation.

Choosing Which Audiovisuals to Use

Here are some types of audiovisuals to consider:

- Object that you use to focus attention or make a point
- Posters
- Flip charts
- White boards
- Overhead transparency projectors
- Slide projectors
- A short video clip or segment
- A short audio clip of a speech, interview, or song

- Computer presentation graphics such as PowerPoint
- Handouts (you may not think of these as audiovisuals, but they are visuals)

With audiovisuals, simpler is usually better, especially for the occasional speaker who wants to form a connection with the audience. Here are some guidelines for choosing which audiovisuals to use (if any):

For speeches (in contrast to workshops and seminars), keep the focus on your speech and connecting with the audience. Use white boards, overheads, flip charts, or presentation graphics only if they add significantly to the impact of your presentation. These kinds of peripherals can complicate your presentation, call attention away from you as a person, and evoke a classroom atmosphere that emphasizes imparting information rather than new ways of thinking. I recently attended an evening program for parents of teens presented by the director of an alcohol and substance abuse treatment program. He used no visuals at all. In fact, he sat in the middle of a group of 100 people. He mostly told stories and answered questions. His presentation was far more effective than if he had used overheads on "how to tell if your child is using drugs." He connected with the audience as a person and an expert, rather than as someone giving parents the latest facts about drugs.

If you can make your point more vivid and memorable with an object, do so. I still remember my high school baccalaureate speaker's use of maple tree seed pods (the little "helicopters") as a way to symbolize how we would be scattered in many different directions, often far from the tree that gave us birth, but that our purpose was to take root and grow wherever we found ourselves.

If you only have a limited number of visual images or charts to present, consider using a poster. A mounted poster is easier to handle than a flip chart and paper. It can be put aside after you've made your point or mounted on a stand if you want to continue referring to it. A mounted poster will stay in good condition through many speeches whereas flip chart paper wears out fairly quickly. Unless you can create a professional-looking poster yourself, consider asking an artist or professional sign maker to prepare the poster for you.

Flip charts work well with fairly small groups (25–30 maximum), especially if you are involving the participants and their input in the process. Flip charts are difficult for everyone to see when used with larger groups. If you are using flip charts to make your own points, prepare the pages in advance—people lose interest when watching you write out your points. In training situations, flip charts can provide some variety if you alternate between making certain points on overhead transparencies and others on flip charts.

Overhead transparency projectors have several advantages over flip charts for *presenting* information. Some of their advantages are:

- Transparencies, unlike flip charts, can be prepared using computer word processors or graphic presentation programs such as PowerPoint.
- You can write directly on the transparencies during the presentations to make points and can erase or correct the marks then or afterward as long as you use erasable markers.
- You can turn overhead projectors on and off as needed during the presentation so they don't distract the audience when not in use.
- You can adjust the size of the projected images to fit the size of the audience and room.
- You can use the transparencies many times and replace individual transparencies if they need revising.
- With computer presentation programs such as PowerPoint, you can easily produce printed handouts of your overhead transparencies.

You may choose to use slide projectors if you want to use photographs, charts, or diagrams to make your points. An example would be a presentation on body language in which you use photographs to demonstrate different stances. One problem with slide projectors is that they usually require the lights to be dimmed to see the slides clearly. This can make it harder for people to stay awake. You may also fade into the background and become a disembodied voice in the darkness.

PowerPoint and similar graphic presentation programs can be used to produce a professional-looking program that you can revise easily to fit each audience. Some speakers rely on PowerPoint images, slides, and overheads to serve as their "notes" so that they don't lose their place or forget a major point. Unfortunately, presentations that rely on PowerPoint for their content are seldom as engaging as presentations that use PowerPoint to supplement what the speaker is saying. If you use slides, make sure you have checked and double-checked the slides and the equipment. Misspellings and out-of-order or upside-down slides can quickly detract from your presentation and your credibility. PowerPoint makes possible special effects and simple animations to keep interest. Be careful not to overdo the special effects; they can become distracting. You are giving an informative presentation, not a "light and laser" multimedia show.

VCRs make it possible to show short segments of video fairly reliably as long as you are working with a small audience or have multiple monitors all connected to the VCR. Examples might be clips of interactions between people or clips from television programs that you use to make your points.

Audio recordings (cassette tapes, CDs, or minidisks) can be used to get attention or make a point. I have seen speakers begin speeches by playing part of a song or part of an old-time radio show. If you were giving a speech on business communication, you might play recordings of simulated conversations to demonstrate styles of interactions or types of conflicts.

For every presentation, you must weigh the possible advantages of using audiovisuals with the risk that they will detract for the reasons mentioned or because the equipment doesn't work properly. Always ask yourself, "Do I need audio-visuals to do a professional job, or can I present the information as easily in handouts?" We will discuss ways to use handouts in Chapter 8, "Keeping Your Presentations Working for You."

Tips for Using Audiovisuals Effectively

Remember that audiovisuals can add impact to your presentation, but they are not the presentation itself. At most, they should supplement your speech.

Practice using your audiovisuals until you are completely comfortable with them. Be prepared to give your presentation without audiovisuals in case something goes wrong. Cue up any tapes and check sound levels by making sure the sound can be heard in all parts of the room. Take a spare of anything that could wear out, run out, or get lost: projector bulbs, markers, and blank transparencies, for example.

Use your own equipment, if possible, to reduce surprises. If you will be using the organization's equipment, check and double-check that everything will be there and be what you need. One speaker had been assured that the organization had an overhead projector, but she discovered to her dismay that not all overhead projectors accept a full-size 8 1/2 x 11" transparency. She had to make do with transparencies that were too big for the projector throughout a 4-hour workshop she was leading.

Do not talk *while* you are writing on a board, flip chart, or overhead transparency. Refer to the screen, but be certain to face the audience whenever speaking. This is important both for sound and for audience contact. Watch television weathercasters to see how they do this.

Pause briefly after moving to a new slide or transparency to let the audience take it in. Do not read to your audience from a projected image or flip chart. Summarize what it says, let them read it, and then talk about what it means or why it is important. If you are using projected images during only part of your presentation, blank the image or turn off the projector during the rest of the presentation so the images do not distract attention from what you are saying.

Using Microphones

Even though you will not need a microphone for smaller gatherings, learning to use microphones and public address amplifiers will pay dividends with groups of 50 or more. Many civic organizations that meet regularly will use amplifiers.

Microphones usually fall into one of the following categories, with their own characteristics and user tips.

- *Wired podium-mounted microphones.* The disadvantage of a podium-mounted microphone is that you cannot walk away from the podium without losing amplification. The sound may fall off just from turning your head too far to one side. But it is often the only choice you have. If you must use a mounted microphone, adjust the height and direction so it is pointing directly at your mouth when you are in your normal speaking position. (Many speakers adjust the mic when they are standing at the podium. When they start to speak, they lean forward and down toward their notes, leaving the microphone pointed at their forehead.) Also make sure the amplifier is set high enough to pick up your voice in your natural speaking volume, but not so high that it creates feedback or hum. You may be able to remove a wired mounted microphone from its stand, allowing you to walk around within the limits of the cord. Make sure the mic has a very long cord and you have practiced avoiding getting tangled in the cord before you start walking into the audience carrying a corded mic with you. Many a speaker has made a memorable speech, not because of what he said, but because he entertained his distracted audience by getting tangled again and again in the mic cord.

- *Wireless handheld microphones.* These can also be placed in a stand on the podium. The advantages of a wireless handheld mic is that you can move around, carrying it with you. You can also adjust the direction and distance from your mouth to get optimal sound and volume. The disadvantage is that it leaves only one hand free to hold notes and gesture. You also have to remember to hold the mic in position instead of gesturing and pointing with it.

- *Wireless lavaliere or lapel microphones.* These microphones are probably the favorite of most speakers because they allow you to move around and almost forget about the microphone. You just have to make sure to clip it so it will pick up your voice without amplifying the sound of your clothing or jewelry rubbing against it. With all wireless microphones, you also need to make sure you have fresh batteries. Many speakers pack extra 9-volt, C, and AA batteries in their bag in case the wireless mic batteries give out partway through their presentation.

❏ PLANNING IN ADVANCE FOR THE UNEXPECTED

Sometimes, despite all our preparation, something goes wrong. If you have thought about how to handle problems, you can relax and be much more effective if something does go awry. One way to prepare for mechanical problems is to bring spare supplies and equipment, as we've suggested. If possible, have a technical support person on call to help with equipment problems that occur.

Problems can be divided into two types: (a) those that affect the audience (that the audience would be aware of) and (b) those that only affect you (you start to feel sick, etc.) .If the problem is something that affects the audience (equipment, lights, major distraction), it is best to acknowledge it. If you are comfortable making a joke about it, do so. For example: The electric power goes out: "I guess the power company really meant it when they said: Final Notice." Or a projector bulb dies: "Why is it that the more you pay for a bulb, the shorter it lasts? My nightlight bulb runs all night for 7 years. This one is 2 weeks old."

More important, see if you can get someone to fix it. If it is something as simple as the kitchen staff making too much noise in the room next door, you can say: "Could someone ask them to please hold it down so we can have our meeting?"

If the problem will take a little longer to fix (as in a lighting or sound problem), you could ask the audience some questions. Another option is to make light of it:

"Who else has had something go wrong today? Would you like to get it off your chest?" Or "Who's had something go *right* today? Would you be willing to tell us about it?" Be careful with the humorous approach, however. It can completely change the mood you want to establish when you resume speaking.

If you are the only one who can fix the problem (your projector bulb burns out, for example), give the audience a topic or question to discuss with one another while you are busy solving the problem. If the problem can't be corrected, decide whether it is better to go ahead as best you can (without audiovisuals, for example) or reschedule it for another time.

If the problem is something going on with you, such as losing your place, feeling sick, or a dry throat, consider the following. If it is a temporary lapse of memory, just acknowledge it. Humorous: "Can anybody tell me what I was saying before my mind left me just now?" Matter of fact: "Where was I?" or simply pause to check your notes. If you make a gaff, mistake, or faux pas: Simply apologize and say it right: "Excuse me. I meant to say: _____." Or make light of it: "You'll have to excuse me, but sometimes my mouth has a mind of its own." Or "I wish I could tell you I said that just to see if you were paying attention, but I'm not even sure what I said myself." Or "Sugar affects me that way sometimes!" If you feel sick: Pause, take a deep breath or two, and sip some water to see if it will pass quickly. If you need to stop briefly to go to the restroom, for example, here are some options: Tell them you've had a bug or have been taking medication that upsets your system. "I'll be back in about 2 minutes and in the meantime I want you to turn to the person next to you and talk about _____ (what you've learned that's new, what questions you have for me, how you've handled a problem like the ones we're talking about, etc.)."

In most cases you will be able to go on and finish your presentation. If not, tell the audience that you are suddenly feeling ill and you will need to stop. They will understand.

❏ KNOWING HOW TO SHORTEN THE PRESENTATION

We talked about ways to end your presentation in the last chapter. Knowing how you will end is like knowing exactly what exit you will take on the interstate. If you know clearly what you are going to do, you do not have to worry about whether you will miss it or get lost.

Sometimes, you have to cut your presentation shorter than intended. You may have started later than planned because of other items on the agenda. Maybe you spent too much time on one section or had more audience participation than you expected. Whatever the reason, how do you cut it short? What you should *not* do is talk faster and faster or start summarizing everything in a general way, trying to cover everything. Your audience will tune out.

If you do not have time to cover everything, cut something short rather than rush to include everything. This is easier to do on the spur of the moment if you have thought in advance about what points are most essential. If your presentation is a tree with a main trunk, three large branches, and then smaller branches coming off the three large branches, you should not cut the trunk or the three large branches. The speech may not make sense if you do. Instead, cut some of the smaller branches, or state them without elaborating. The audience will still get your main points.

If you have three examples to illustrate a point, use one or two instead of all three. If one of your three points is easy to understand without explanation, and not as important as your other points, state the point without elaborating. Use fewer details in telling a story. If you have covered something in your handout, make the point and say: "You can read more about that in the handout you received." If you're speaking to a business or professional group and need to cut something short, you can say: "Let me give you the executive summary on this." Then give them the main points without elaboration.

Another option is to make a point briefly and offer to provide more resources after the talk to anyone who wants more information about that point. You could say, if you're willing: "If you want to know more than we've been able to cover in this short explanation, ask me afterward or send me an e-mail and I'll direct you to some additional resources."

Don't be afraid to tell the audience that you are giving them less detail on certain points because you want to honor the time limits. Audiences may wish you would have talked longer, but that's much better than their wishing you had not spoken so long.

❏ ALLOWING TIME FOR QUESTIONS AND ANSWERS

A question-and-answer period allows people to ask about what they are most interested in or concerned about as well as anything they did not understand. If you handle it well, a question-and-answer period can also give the audience more of a sense of what you are like as a person.

The simplest way to handle questions is to have people stand and ask their questions. In very large groups, it may work better to have people write out their questions and pass them forward. The main advantage of the latter approach is that you can choose the questions you want to answer and avoid having people take too much time by making a speech of their own.

If people are asking their own questions, here are a few pointers:

- Repeat the question so that everyone knows what you are responding to.
- If you are not sure whether you understood the question, ask if you have it right or ask them to clarify what they are asking.
- Direct your attention to the person who is asking the question. Speak directly to the questioner with the first part of your answer. Then, if your answer applies more broadly, you can expand your attention to others in the audience.
- If possible, walk away from the podium and toward the audience during the question-and-answer period. This is an excellent opportunity to engage with them and become even more

real and approachable. You may not be able to do this if the microphone is attached to the podium.

- Avoid arguing with questioners. Sometimes questioners will be confrontational, but you will only lose if you become confrontational in return. If possible, acknowledge that they feel strongly about their position and that your point of view is simply different. Sometimes you can show empathy and say that you would be glad to talk further with them afterward.

- Whatever you do, do not put the questioner down in any way, no matter how irritated you may be.

CHAPTER 7

Managing Your Fear

IF YOU ARE ANXIOUS about public speaking, you are not alone. A frequently quoted survey found that more people reported being afraid of public speaking than being afraid of dying. Performance anxiety is not all negative. Some anxiety helps us do our best. Anxiety makes us prepare well. Because of anxiety, we may approach the presentation with a sense of excitement.

If we were not at all anxious in advance, we would probably not do as well as if we are moderately anxious. A consultant friend recently told me about making a presentation to a group of prospective clients. He had felt surprisingly calm about the whole thing beforehand, and he did poorly. He had not adequately understood the prospects' concerns and had given a presentation that missed the mark. They were not interested in doing business with him. He realized afterward that because he was not anxious, he had not prepared as carefully as usual. He had not checked out the audience's interests in advance. He had seen it as "no big deal."

Our goal in doing effective presentations is not to eliminate our anxiety, but to manage it. We need enough anxiety that we prepare adequately and seek to do our best without feeling overwhelmed by the fear and dread that many speakers feel. Ideally, the anxiety we feel is motivating, not debilitating.

How can you learn to manage your fear of public speaking? The methods I will teach you in this chapter are the most effective techniques I have found in years of study, experience, and teaching. Some of them may sound simple, but each is a powerful antidote to the fear that many feel about public speaking. None of these methods will work without application and practice. And no one of these methods will necessarily work by itself, without the others, to transform your fear. But if you take time to learn and apply these methods for yourself, I believe they can have a profound effect on your speaking.

We do not fully understand why public speaking is so widely feared. The fears most reported involve a fear of being criticized, a fear of being humiliated or making a fool of oneself, and a fear of being put on the spot in front of other people.

We know that for many people the greatest fear comes as they anticipate speaking to a group. They may be anxious throughout the preparation, with the highest anxiety coming just before they walk to the podium to begin. Many speakers report that within a minute or two after they begin, most of their anxiety has vanished.

One reason the fear of speaking persists for so many is that they avoid public speaking whenever possible. Lacking the skills you will learn in this chapter and lacking the experience of speaking except under stress and duress, many people perpetuate their fear because when they do speak they are fearful and may not do a particularly effective job. Lacking tools to reduce their anxiety, they are often paralyzed by fear during the preparation process and do not adequately get ready for the presentation. The following recommendations for learning to manage fear of speaking are designed to change that pattern.

❏ GETTING EXPERIENCE SPEAKING IN LOW-RISK SITUATIONS

You will not become less fearful of public speaking without doing some public speaking, so start by finding places to speak that have less risk for you than speaking to a large group you do not know. By "low risk" I mean situations where there would be few if any negative consequences for losing your train of thought, being nervous, or whatever else you may fear about speaking.

The lowest-risk speaking situation is an empty room at your home or office. If you are anxious about speaking, start giving short presentations by yourself. What good can it possibly do if there are no other people present? you may ask. What speaking to an empty room can do is give you some experience of speaking without being afraid. It can also allow you to experiment with your voice, with your body, and with language. It is a little like learning to sing better by first singing in the shower. Pretend you are giving a speech and make it up as you go. Later in this chapter you will learn the practice of speaking to one person at a time. When speaking to the empty room, pretend that you are speaking to one person who is interested in and supportive of what you have to say. Imagine it is your best friend or your most loyal supporter.

If you have been avoiding public speaking, look for ways to get experience in groups where you are known and where the stakes are low. Make announcements, give reports, introduce visitors, or express your point of view in your committee meetings, civic groups, parent meetings, or religious organization.

Another low-risk speaking situation is Toastmasters, a self-help organization with local meetings where people who want to improve their public speaking skills practice speaking to others like themselves. Toastmasters meetings follow a structured format designed to give participants as much experience and feedback as possible in a supportive atmosphere. This organization has probably helped more people than any other learn to manage their fear and improve their effectiveness in public speaking. See their listing in the Resources section at the back of the book.

If you have little speaking experience, you may want to offer your first "real" presentation to a small group—a parents group or a class, for example. You can also ask a few friends or colleagues if they would let you practice your first presentation on them.

❑ NOTICING AND COUNTERACTING ANXIOUS THOUGHTS

If the idea of speaking makes you highly nervous, spend time noticing what you say to yourself about it. Notice what thoughts and beliefs contribute to this "self talk." The process of becoming aware of underlying thoughts and beliefs works best if you write down the thoughts as you notice them.

Here are examples of thoughts and beliefs that my clients and I have had:

"The audience is not going to like me."
"I don't have anything interesting to say."
"If I mess up, I will be humiliated."
"I have to do it perfectly."
"What if I forget what I was going to say?"
"What if the audience gets bored?"
"I'm not good enough as a speaker."
"I will be so nervous, I won't be able to talk."
"The audience will make fun of me when they see how nervous I am or when I make a mistake."
"People will discover that I don't know what I'm doing."
"Unless I do a perfect job, it will be a disaster."
"My future rests on this presentation, so I don't dare screw up."
"The other speakers they've had are much better than I am."
"I won't be prepared enough."
"What I have to say isn't worth their time."

Often we are not aware of this kind of self talk until we stop and notice it. But the effects of these thoughts and beliefs are powerful, whether we are consciously aware of them or not. We think we are anxious because of the situation we are in, but to a large degree we are scaring ourselves by what we are telling ourselves about the situation. If I keep telling myself that what I am doing is scary and dangerous, I will become more frightened than if I tell myself that what I am doing is new to me but something I am able to do.

For many, including myself, speaking sometimes seems like walking blindfolded along a long narrow board. Doing so is not always easy and we often have to feel our way. What makes speaking scary is our believing and telling ourselves that it is as though the board is suspended 100 feet above the ground so that one misstep will be disastrous. In reality, the board is 6 inches off the ground and if we lose our footing, we can step right back on without injury and keep going. But as long as we believe that the board is 100 feet above the ground, we will be terrified of failure.

What can you do about your negative thoughts once you become aware of them? There are several helpful methods for dealing with negative thinking. One approach, based on cognitive-behavioral therapy is to identify the cognitive distortions or mistruths in your thoughts and beliefs, and then counteract the distortions with more accurate or constructive thoughts or beliefs. David Burns (1999) identifies 10 main types of cognitive distortions:[*]

1. All-or-nothing thinking: You see everything in terms of black-and-white categories. If your presentation is not outstanding, it is a complete failure.

2. Overgeneralization: You view a single action or event as always being true. If you occasionally lose your place in a presentation, you conclude that you "are always losing your place."

3. Mental filter: You view everything through the distorted perspective of one negative detail. If you do not like the sound of your voice, you convince yourself that it doesn't really matter what you say because your voice will spoil your speech anyway.

4. Disqualifying the positive: You dismiss positive experiences because they "don't count" for some reason, thus holding on to your negative belief. Even though many people tell you they enjoy your presentation, you find reasons why their opinion doesn't count (they aren't experts, they're just being nice, other people didn't like it, etc.).

5. Jumping to conclusions: You come to a negative conclusion even though there is no real evidence to support your interpretation. A few people left before you finished your presentation, so you conclude that they left because they were bored and that therefore your presentation was boring.

    a. Mind reading: You interpret someone's reaction to you negatively without checking out what they think. Someone in

---

[*] Ten Cognitive Distortions list is from *Feeling Good: The New Mood Therapy* (pp. 49–50) by David D. Burns, M.D. ©Copyright 1980 David D. Burns, M.D. Reprinted by permission of HaperCollins, Inc. William Morrow.

the front row looked angry through your whole presentation, so you conclude he did not like what you were saying.

b. The fortune-teller error: You are convinced that something will go wrong even though you have no evidence for your prediction. You say to yourself: "I know they are not going to like me."

6. Magnification (catastrophizing) or minimization: You exaggerate or underestimate the effect of something you do. You give a subpar presentation and you convince yourself that it means you will never be invited to speak in that city again.

7. Emotional reasoning: You conclude that the way you are feeling is a reflection of way things are. You feel bad about your presentation, so you conclude that means you did a bad job.

8. Should statements: You create a demand on yourself to do something so that you will feel guilty if you do not do it. "I should accept this speaking invitation even though it really is inconvenient, given my schedule."

9. Labeling and mislabeling: you apply a negative label to yourself. "I'm a loser." Or "I'm a bore." Or "I'm hopeless."

10. Personalization: You blame yourself for something that you are not actually responsible for. You are late for a meeting because the program chairperson was confused about the time and gave you the wrong information. You blame yourself for not knowing the correct time.

Using Burns's (1999) cognitive-behavioral approach, you would identify the distortion in your underlying self talk, and then counteract with a more accurate, undistorted thought or statement. Writing out your self talk and counteracting thoughts is usually more effective than just thinking about it.

Here are a few examples:

EXAMPLE 7.1. Self talk: "I don't have anything interesting to say."

Cognitive distortion(s): All or nothing; overgeneralization; emotional reasoning; disqualifying the positive (could be any or all of these).

Counteracting, accurate statement: I may be setting a very high standard for myself. If I give the audience information that helps them understand and think about the topic in a new way, they will probably find it interesting. I will make sure I get the audience involved in the presentation as well.

EXAMPLE 7.2. Self talk: "Unless I do a perfect job, it will be a disaster."

Cognitive distortion(s): All or nothing; jumping to conclusions (fortune-telling); magnification (catastrophizing).

Counteracting, accurate statement: "I do not need to do a perfect job for it to go well. In fact, there is no such thing as a 'perfect' presentation. What I can do is prepare and practice, and plan ways to involve the audience so that I'm sure to connect it to their interests. I will also plan in advance for ways to handle the things that could go wrong."

EXAMPLE 7.3. Self talk: "I will be so nervous I won't be able to talk."

Cognitive distortion(s): Mental filter; jumping to conclusions (fortune-telling).

Counteracting, accurate statement: "I may be nervous, especially beforehand and at the beginning. Even though I really dislike how I feel before a presentation, my nervousness mostly goes away once I get started. I will practice speaking with one person at a time and I will focus on what I want to get across to the audience. That and the rest of what I am learning will enable me to manage my fear."

Another method for dealing with thoughts and beliefs is an approach developed by Bryon Katie (2002). She recommends taking the thoughts and beliefs you identify and asking the following questions one at a time:[*]

1. "Is it true?"
2. "Can you absolutely know that it's true?"

---

[*] From *Loving What Is* by Byron Katie and Stephen Mitchell, ©Copyright 2002 by Byron Katie and Stephen Mitchell. Used by permission of Harmony Books, a division of Random House, Inc.

3.   "How do you react when you think that thought?"
4.   "Who would you be without the thought?"

Then she suggests what she calls "turning it around" to see in what ways the converse statement is also true.

Here is an example using the thought "What I have to say isn't worth their time."

1.   "Is it true?" Probably not, although I still feel this way. If I give them some helpful information and new ways of thinking about the topic, it will probably be worthwhile.
2.   "Can you absolutely know that it's true?" No.
3.   "How do you react when you think that thought?" I feel myself pulling back, closing down, and feeling smaller. I find it harder to think clearly about what I want to say.
4.   "Who would you be without the thought?" I would be freer, more confident, better able to decide what will be helpful to the audience. I would not need to hold back.

Now I'll "turn it around" and see how the converse is true: Original thought: "What I have to say isn't worth their time." The "turned around" thought: "It is worth their time to hear what I have to say." How is this true? In truth, everyone can learn something helpful from my presentation. I can't control their reaction, but if they are open, they will probably find it worthwhile. What I need to do is decide what I can do that *will* make it worthwhile for this audience.

Here's another example, using the thought: "Unless I do a perfect job, it will be disaster."

1.   "Is it true?" When I imagine myself being nervous and awkward and ineffective, it *feels* like it will be disastrous.
2.   "Can you absolutely know that it's true?" No, not really. I realize that my disaster fantasies are based on my doing worse than I have ever done in giving a presentation. I've seen other speakers do an average to mediocre job and nobody thinks much about it.

3. "How do you react when you think that thought?" When I imagine my speech as a disaster, I get shaky and want to call the whole thing off. I notice that I use my nervousness as evidence that there is something to be afraid of.

4. "Who would you be without the thought?" I would be motivated to prepare well and do a good job, but I would not be terrified. I would design a presentation that allows me to use my strengths and be myself. I would plan what to do for anything that may go wrong. I would look for ways to turn my excitement into positive energy.

If I "turn it around" what happens? Original thought: "Unless I do a perfect job, it will be a disaster." "Turned around" thought: "If I don't do a perfect job, it will be much better." In what ways is the second statement true? Not doing a perfect job means I can be authentic and real. I can let them see more of me, and I can use the energy that I would have spent trying to be "perfect" to connect with the audience. All of that will definitely make the presentation better than if I try to do a perfect job.

❑ PRACTICING SPEAKING TO ONE PERSON AT A TIME

The single most valuable technique for managing your fear of speaking is to change your view of the presentation from a performance to a conversation, from a speech for 50 or 200 people to a give-and-take with one person at a time. I introduced this approach in the last chapter. Now I want to elaborate in more detail, including more practical techniques for reframing your presentation as a conversation rather than a performance.

When many people stand up in front of a group of 50 or 100 people, they are aware of a sea of faces. Without necessarily being conscious of it, they feel they are supposed to "do something" with each person. As speakers, they try to be aware of all these people at once, and they are overwhelmed. I compare it to trying to throw balls back and forth, to play catch, with everyone in the room all at once. If there were 75 people, you would be trying to play catch with 75 people with 75 balls. You could not do it. But if you were to play catch with one person at a time, throwing and catching just one ball, you could probably imagine doing it without too much anxiety. If you cannot imagine throwing or catching a ball with even one person, imagine exchanging introductions with one person at a time instead of everyone at once.

This same idea extends to thinking about your presentation: When you view it as a conversation or interaction with one person at a time, rather than as having to engage an entire group of people, it becomes something you can do more easily.

Here is another way of describing the presentation process. I imagine I am having a conversation with someone. As I am talking to this person, other people walk up and join the group, and I acknowledge them with my eye contact. But I continue always talking to just one person at a time. I may shift my attention from one person to another, and I trust that the others who are watching will be listening as well. But in my mind, I am never trying to talk with more than one person at a time.

Who is the one person I am talking with? As I look from one person to another, in one sense I am talking with each person in turn. In my mind, however, I am talking with someone who genuinely wants to understand what I have to say, to someone who is interested and curious. Just as athletes picture themselves successfully making a putt or a basket, I imagine myself talking to one individual who wants to learn more about what I have to say. Then, as I look from one person to the next, I imagine that each new person is that person who is interested in what I have to say.

Try this: Think of someone you know who would be interested in learning more about your topic. Choose someone who would be patient, nonjudgmental, and supportive of you, even if you had trouble explaining yourself clearly. Now close your eyes and envision yourself talking with that person about your topic. Picture that person listening to and learning from your presentation. See and hear yourself talking confidently and naturally with this person, asking questions, responding to questions, and explaining the content of your topic.

Notice how you feel in different parts of your body. Notice your thoughts and feelings. Notice especially your positive feelings of confidence and ease. Now make a mental "recording" of how it feels to be talking with this interested, patient, and supportive person. After you open your eyes, let yourself recall the recorded sense of what it is like to talk with this person. See if you can sustain the inner state of talking with this supportive person as you go through the next activities of your day.

Do not expect to be able to do this the first time you try it, and do not be surprised if it feels awkward and difficult the first several times. This is a skill that does not come naturally and is like trying to ride a bicycle when you are just learning. You will be tempted to give up, convinced that you cannot do it. Practice at least twice a day, closing your eyes and imagining speaking with the supportive person you have chosen. As you are able to feel what it would be like to speak more confidently and easily with such a person, mentally record how it feels so you can recall it later. Then practice it at points throughout the day and evening.

If you have trouble speaking easily and naturally with the person you chose to imagine, try the exercise with a different person in mind to see if it works better. The goal of all your practice is to learn to be yourself with the group. The more you are able to do that, the less nervous you will be.

Once you are able to recall the feeling and sense of talking with a supportive person, try recalling this state when you are actually talking with an individual person. Let yourself imagine that the person you are talking with is just like the supportive and interested person you imagined. Imagine this not with your mind, which may resist and find reasons that this is not so. Instead, imagine it by simply recalling how it feels to talk with an interested and supportive person, and let yourself feel these same feelings with the person you are talking with. Notice how it changes your experience of talking with them, and especially how it makes you feel more confident and at ease.

You may be thinking that it is strange, artificial, or gimmicky to imagine you are talking with a supportive, interested person while you are really talking to this real person sitting in front of you. In fact, we are, without realizing it, continually imagining that the person we are talking with is someone else. Often, as speakers, we expect the audience to be critical and disapproving. That is a large reason for our fear. But when we expect that, it is because we are imagining or projecting a critical and disapproving person onto members of the audience and believing it is real. With the method I have just described, you are able to use a positive projection to create a different and more supportive experience.

The other skill to learn is how to talk with one person at a time while shifting your attention from one person to another in a group. The foundation of this skill is learning that you can only speak with one person at a time, as I have suggested. Begin by practicing speaking with one person at a time in a small conversational group, and with practice, you will learn to shift your attention naturally from one person to another.

When you are speaking with a group of 40 or 75 or 300 people, however, and you have material that you want to cover in a particular order, shifting your focus from one person to another can cause you to lose track of what you are saying. You need a way to have the conversations and interactions you are having with this series of people be part of one continuous conversation. Otherwise, shifting from one person to another will feel like an interruption.

The most helpful method I have found is a continuation of the technique where you imagined talking with an interested and supportive person. When I speak to a group of 50 or 75 people, I am really talking with one person at a time whom I actively imagine as an interested and supportive person. This imagining is not a mental exercise, but a recalling and reenacting of the physical sensations and emotional feelings of speaking to the imagined supportive listener.

When I shift my attention from one person to another as I speak, at one level I am aware that each is a different person and I will be aware that this person may have different questions or needs than someone else. At another level, however, I am still talking to the same imagined supportive person when I shift my attention from one person to another. Because of this continuity, I do not experience the shift as a significant disruption or distraction.

In the theater, there is the concept of the fourth wall in which the actors perform as though there is a wall between them and the audience. When they act, as characters they are oblivious to the audience. They do not go out of character or interact with the audience.

In speaking, we must be aware of the audience and interact with them. But if we focus too much on how the audience reacts, and especially with what we imagine their behavior means, we will lose our way as presenters. Holding the sense that we are always speaking to a single individual who is interested and supportive serves a similar function that the concept of the "fourth wall" provides in theater. It allows us to stay centered as speakers rather than becoming overly concerned with the audience reaction.

❏ ENGAGING THE AUDIENCE AROUND YOUR TOPIC

If you focus all your attention on the ideas and information you want to help your audience understand and on how to engage the audience in the process, you will not have room to worry about how well you do or whether the audience will like you. You will focus instead on the question: What points do I want to get across and what are the best ways to do it? You will be considering what you believe will be helpful and interesting to the audience, not how to give an outstanding performance to win your audience's love and approval.

You cannot control the audience's reaction to your presentation. Of course, we often do not realize this. We often think that if we just do a good-enough job (translate that as "outstanding" or "perfect"), the audience will love us. That idea is mistaken.

People in the audience are there for many reasons and with many agendas and issues going on in their lives. Some audience members may be required to attend. Some may have just received bad news or are struggling with a personal crisis. If your presentation is intended to be inspirational, you may not succeed with these people no matter how excellent your talk.

Many in an audience will be "low reactors," which means that they do not show how they are reacting in any way you can sense. You may conclude that that means they are bored or displeased. Usually it does not mean that at all.

With most audiences, a few people will think your presentation was one of the best they have heard. They will love you. A few people will not like your topic, your examples, or your style of speaking. They were wanting something else and you were not it. And most of the audience will think you did fine, OK, satisfactory, very good, or even excellent. Regardless of the reaction you get, it is important to remember that you cannot control their reaction and you certainly cannot win the love and approval of everyone who hears you.

No matter how much preparation you do, you may still feel anxious before or during your presentation, so it will pay to do the following.

❏ LEARNING METHODS FOR HANDLING THE ANXIETY ITSELF

The physical symptoms of anxiety are part of the well-documented "fight or flight" syndrome triggered when we perceive danger or threat. We know them well—the quickened heart and breathing rate, the surge of adrenaline, and the heightened alertness. They can be quite uncomfortable and difficult to tolerate.

Quick ways to reduce the intensity of the anxiety are:

Breathe. Take a breath, tighten your belly like you're preparing to take a punch, then breathe out slowly through your mouth while keeping your abdomen tight. Then let go, relax, and breathe normally. Sarnoff (1997) developed this method of anxiety reduction for speakers after learning that the late actor, Yul Brynner, reduced his stage fright by pushing against a wall with both hands while waiting to go on stage. Any movement that causes a tightening of the abdomen and a slow release of the breath seems to have a similar anxiety-reducing effect. A variation, if you are seated, is to grip the bottom edge of your chair on each side and pull up, tightening your abdominal muscles as you do.

Move. If you are speaking, walk away from the podium and out into the audience, if possible. Gesture or move your hands for emphasis. Since the fight-or-flight reaction is designed to help us move quickly, even a little additional movement can relieve some of the intensity of the feelings.

Stretch. Stretching your arms, legs, and torso helps because you are moving, and stretches also help relieve the tension in your body. In a workshop or informal speaking situation, you could even invite the audience to stretch as a way to relax. They will enjoy it too and they need not know that your real reason for leading the stretch was to help settle your nerves.

Tense and relax. Tightening your muscles and then releasing them is the basic process called progressive relaxation. You can probably tense and relax muscles without anyone noticing while waiting for your turn to speak.

Tap or rub acupressure points. Tapping or rubbing certain acupressure points on the body can quickly reduce tension. One set of these points includes the bone above the eye, the bone to the side of the eye, the bone directly under the eye, the midpoint between the lip and the nose, the midpoint between the lower lip and the chin, the end of the collar bone near the sternum, and the side of the chest about 4 inches below the arm. Gently tapping or rubbing these points, one after the other, can give immediate relief from anxiety. You could rub these points without attracting attention while waiting for your time to speak. If you are speaking on a topic related to stress reduction, you might want to lead the audience in this or other stress reduction exercises as a way of demonstrating your topic at the same time that you lower your own stress.

Focus your attention on something other than your symptoms. One technique you can use while speaking is to make a circle by holding the tips of your thumb and forefinger together. By focusing part of your awareness on holding the circle with your fingers, you take energy and attention away from your anxiety.

Try to *increase* the symptoms of your nervousness by trying to make your heart beat faster, your knees knock more, and so on. Surprisingly, this paradoxical action helps many people be *more* in control and *less* nervous.

Mentally feel yourself occupying the full space in which you are standing. This is an acting method where instead of shrinking inwardly you let yourself expand psychically to fill the space immediately around you. Instead of only taking up the actual space of your physical body, you consciously occupy the area around you up to a foot in each direction. Try doing it first when you are in a conversation, in a meeting, or at a party. Notice how you feel. Many people report feeling more confident and more centered.

Reframe the sensations of anxiety as energy and excitement. Physiologically, fear and excitement are very similar. The main difference is whether we perceive a situation as positive or dangerous. When you notice the sensations and say to yourself, "I am excited about giving this presentation," you can shift the symptoms' effects from something to be avoided to something that can help you do well.

Remember that the audience can only see what is visible. They cannot see your racing mind or your fear of failing. In workshops and coaching, I have videotaped presentations of many people who felt very nervous, especially at the beginning. When they watched the videotape later, they were amazed at how little, if any, of the nervousness was visible. They were also pleasantly surprised that what had felt like awkward moments in the presentation were barely noticeable when they were viewed on the tape.

❏ PREPARING AND PRACTICING FOR A GOOD PRESENTATION

In tandem with the other methods for reducing your anxiety, the final key for managing your fear is preparation and practice. By preparing and practicing, you will discover in advance the places that need more work, rather than finding out in front of the audience that an example is not clear or that your points are not in the right sequence. By practicing, you will become familiar enough with your points and your stories that your notes can be a support and a reminder rather than a script. By practicing, you will stand in front of the audience and know that you have given this presentation several times before.

I have seen many people learn to manage their fear of speaking. They did not all learn to love speaking (although some did), but they did stop avoiding it. Perhaps the greatest benefit that they expressed is the new freedom and confidence they feel in overcoming something they had felt embarrassed or ashamed about. Anyone can learn to manage their fear of speaking by using the methods outlined here and getting experience in a low-risk, safe setting. It almost always feels like a risk in the beginning. It always feels like a victory afterward.

CHAPTER 8

Keeping Your Presentations Working for You

In addition to giving a good presentation and engaging with the audience, you can ensure that the speech achieves the results of greater exposure, increased opportunities for service, and more referrals. This chapter will detail ways that you can make your presentations keep working for you.

❏ GIVING PEOPLE WAYS TO REMEMBER YOU

No matter how good your presentation, unless people receive something with your name and contact information on it, most will forget who you are. You may be able to leave a practice brochure or business card on every chair or on a table where interested people can pick them up. Sometimes, however, the organization to whom you are speaking discourages any actions that could be viewed as self-promoting of your business or practice. Check with the program chairperson to see what would be acceptable. An excellent way to get around the issue of self-promotion, and still make sure everyone has your name and contact information, is to always use handouts when you give a presentation and to have your contact information printed clearly on the handouts.

❏ HOW TO USE HANDOUTS

The purpose of your handout is twofold: (a) to help the audience remember what you said, and (b) to help them remember you, your name, and how to contact you.

Here are types of handouts to consider:

- An outline or an elaboration of the key points you make.
- A copy of your PowerPoint presentation.
- A list of resources, Web sites, books, tips, things to do, things to avoid, biggest mistakes, quotations, or the like.
- A self-scoring assessment or quiz related to the topic. Common examples are stress level or life balance assessments.
- A certificate or prescription that fits in with the point of your talk. A coach could hand out a certificate or "prescription" that is "good for 1 hour spent doing something you really enjoy."
- A wallet or pocket card describing the steps of a process or key elements you talk about in your presentation. Examples could be a relaxation or stress reduction process, steps in resolving a conflict or negotiating an agreement, steps for making good decisions, and so on. You could laminate the card if you have something that people will want to keep (laminating will make it less likely that they will throw it away, although it will also add to your expense).
- A flyer about an upcoming workshop or seminar you will be giving, a calendar about other presentations you will be giving (if some are open to the public), or a flyer or order form for your books, tapes, or other resources. Again, check with your contact person to make sure these are appropriate. Most organizations view information about books, tapes, and workshops as a service to the members who may want to know more.
- A copy of an article that you have written on a topic related to your presentation.
- A letter or certificate offering a complimentary introductory consultation or assessment. If you decide to offer this kind of

incentive, check with the program chairperson first to make sure it would be appropriate with this organization.

Put your name and phone number on every page of anything you hand out at your presentations. If you have a Web site, include the Web site address. If you want to include the contact information, but want to avoid it looking like an advertisement, use your practice letterhead and print the outline on it. If you use plain paper, add one of the following at the top or bottom of the page:

For more information, contact [your name] at (555) 555-5678.
Compliments of [your name] Phone: (555) 555-5678.
Copyright 200_ [your name]. For more information, contact [your name] at (555) 555-5555. www.your website.com

❏ WHEN TO USE HANDOUTS

When should you distribute handouts? If the handouts are outlines that will help the audiences follow your organization and perhaps take notes, distribute the handouts at the beginning or put them at every place or on every chair before people arrive. If the handouts are supplements to your presentation but give additional information beyond what you are presenting, consider giving them to audience members at the end so they do not read them during your talk instead of listening to you.

If you have more than one or two handouts, consider putting them in a pocket folder and giving one to each person. By using pocket folders, you can usually include a practice brochure and business card along with the educational handouts without raising the flag of self-promotion. A variation on giving a folder to everyone is to have a handout for everyone and offer packets for those who are particularly interested in learning more about the topic. This can reduce costs and waste, but it also runs the risk that a potential client or referral source might not learn more about you.

❑ GETTING MAXIMUM REFERRAL POSSIBILITIES

If one of your reasons for speaking is to build your coaching or psychotherapy practice, you will want to do what you can to elicit positive response by those who might want to use your services or to refer others to you. Here are some keys to improving the response to your presentation.

Prepare well so you can do a good job. Think of your presentation as an audition for possible clients. The better impression you make, the more likely you will generate interest among prospective clients for your services. You do not have to be a great speaker to make a good impression, but you do need to be prepared, reasonably clear and thoughtful, and able to engage the audience.

Tell stories that subtly describe how you work with your clients. Since part of your purpose is building your practice, include at least one reference to your work with clients. For example: "Many of the clients I work with. . . ." or "One of my clients was facing this problem. . . ." As a psychotherapist or coach, you need to be clear that you have changed the details of any examples to protect their confidentiality.

Show that you respect your clients and have compassion for their struggles. Never speak disparagingly about clients in any examples you use. A rule of thumb I use is this: If my clients were sitting in the audience, they would not be uncomfortable with what I said and how I described the situation. Prospective clients in the audience will be judging you not only as a speaker but also as someone they can trust.

Allow time for a question-and-answer period near the end of your presentation. I cannot overemphasize the value of this. This is how you make sure you deal with the audience's specific questions and concerns. This is when the audience gets to see more of the real you and not just the speech you have prepared. This is also when you get a chance to connect more closely with individual members of the audience. For more suggestions on how to handle questions effectively, refer to Chapter 6.

Make it clear that you will be glad to stay afterward if people have specific questions. Tell them where you will be if they want to ask questions. For example, "I will stick around near the back of the room as long as anyone has questions." Or "I would love a chance to speak to each one of you, so I hope you will come up to the podium afterward and say hello."

Be careful about answering questions too quickly. If anyone approaches you afterward with a question or problem, ask more about their situation or problem. Tell them how you might approach the situation rather than give them a definitive answer. More than showing attendees what you know, you want them to see how you relate to people. There is often a temptation when you are in the role of "expert" to give answers rather than to draw the person out. Instead of assuming the role of advice-giver, try turning the conversation into a miniconsultation.

Try not to spend too much time with any one person. If you sense that someone is a potential client, and others are waiting to speak to you, ask if he or she can stay to continue the conversation until you have spoken to the others who are waiting.

❑ HAVING A NEXT STEP FOR PEOPLE WHO WANT MORE

Most people in the audience will probably be encountering you for the first time. Although someone may approach you afterward or call you the next day and say, "I want to set up an appointment to work with you," that will probably not be the typical pattern.

More often, people who are interested will want to learn more or test the waters in a gradual way. You need to have one or more "next steps" that can make sense for people at different stages of additional interest. One next step may be sending them an article or report for them to read. Another might be having them learn more about you and your approach by going to your Web site. A next step may be to offer an additional phone or in-person conversation besides what you can have at the end of a presentation.

If you give other presentations or conduct seminars, workshops, or teleclasses, those can be easy next steps. The reason a seminar, workshop, or teleclass is often a particularly good next step is that it not only gives a person more exposure to you and your approach, but it requires an action on their part. One of the mistakes that some beginning (and experienced) coaches make is to keep doing things for a prospective client, such as sending them information, answering questions, and doing pro bono coaching, without the other person taking any initiative themselves. Signing up for and attending a class or workshop takes initiative that shows some genuine interest.

Another next step for some speakers is to offer a complimentary behavioral assessment such as the DISC. (The DISC is a four-factor assessment so named because it assesses dominance, influence, steadiness, and compliance.) It can be an excellent way to have a longer conversation with someone, to give them a sense of what it could be like to work with you, and for you to test their interest.

Many coaches offer a 30-minute initial complementary telephone coaching session to give someone an experience of what coaching is like and to see whether they feel comfortable with you. Psychotherapists are more divided about whether a no-cost initial session is appropriate. Some therapists believe that people will not value what they do not pay for and that offering free services would detract from their professional image. As a practical consideration, if your practice is almost full and you have few available client openings, it would make less sense to offer no-fee sessions than if you are just starting your practice and have many unfilled hours available.

❏ FOLLOWING UP WITH MEMBERS OF THE AUDIENCE

Handouts and information packets make it easy for the audience to remember and follow up with you if they choose. Depending on your objectives, you may want to find ways to follow up with members of the audience. One way is to offer to send an additional article, report, or presentation outline to anyone who is interested. If someone is interested, all they have to do is give you a business card and write "report" or "article" on the back. Then you will send them a copy. This has several advantages: It encourages people with an interest in your subject to express interest. You get their name and address to follow up. You communicate by your offer that you are a helpful person and an expert. If you are a coach or working in a business context, you may even choose to make a follow-up call to make sure they received the report and to ask them more about their interest. The main point is to give them something they are likely to keep or pass on to someone else that has all of your contact information on it (name and telephone number especially).

Why would you want to take the extra time and expense to do this? The main reason is that you get to establish an ongoing conversation with the people who are especially interested in the topic. You give them another chance to think about you and your topic, to reinforce the connection. You have a way to ensure future exposure with these members of the audience who may decide a year from now that they or people they know need your services. If you have a way to keep your name and contact information in front of them regularly, you greatly increase the chances that they will think of you when they decide they have a need.

Some coaches who speak do a drawing at the end of the presentation. The prize may be a copy of the speaker's book, a cassette or CD, or a copy of someone else's book if they have not written one of their own. To enter the drawing, audience members pass in their business cards or completed feedback forms. Audience members get a chance to win a prize. The speaker gets completed feedback forms, as well as the names and addresses with whom they can follow up with a thank you or other information. If a speaker intends to add these names to a mailing list, that should be announced before the drawing: "If you are interested in the drawing, pass your business card to the aisles and we'll have them collected. I'd like to put you on my mailing list and if you'd rather not be included, just write NO LIST on your card. My e-zine comes out once a month and has lots of practical tips, but it also tells you how to unsubscribe easily. I don't like spam any more than the rest of you, so your name and address will never be given or sold to anyone." If you ask for names and addresses on the feedback sheet, include a box people can check if they want to be included on your mailing list. We will discuss the logistics of mailing lists, newsletters, and e-zines (electronic magazines or newsletters) in Chapter 10.

If you do nothing else to follow up, at least write a thank-you note to the person who arranged for you to speak and with the president of the organization. If you offered to send additional information (reports or presentation notes, for example), send them promptly. In our culture, people tend to generalize about people who follow up promptly by assuming that they are competent. Following up with a thank-you note should be a priority. Why send notes like this when they will probably be sending you a thank-you note for speaking? Because you want to positively reinforce the contact while it is fresh. Someone has said that referral lists are written in "disappearing ink," and people will soon forget about you if you do not reinforce yourself in their memory. Follow-up notes need not take more than five minutes to write, but could lead to a referral or a new client. Human nature is that people like to be remembered and appreciated, and your note will make you stand out in their minds. If you keep a supply of reports and stationery, you can do it the next day while waiting for your next appointment. Some speakers use distinguished-looking postcards with their name and contact information tastefully printed across the top. They can then write quick notes to people they have met and spoken with at speeches. A handwritten note like this can be more effective than a typed letter because it feels more personal.

❏ POSITIONING YOURSELF FOR MORE PRESENTATIONS

One way that a presentation can keep working for you is for it to lead to more speaking engagements. You can increase the chances of that happening by making sure people know you are available to speak. You can include in your biography and introduction the fact that you are a speaker or are available for presentations. In following up afterward with program chairpersons, say that you hope they will give your name to anyone they know who may be looking for speakers.

If the program chairpersons or presidents seemed enthusiastic about your speech, ask if they would be willing to write those things in a short letter of endorsement for you that you can then use as part of your promotional materials. If you are starting out as a speaker, tell them that you are starting to do more speeches and that you would appreciate a letter that you could use in assuring other groups that you can do a good job for them. Program chairpersons are usually glad to do this favor for a speaker who they liked, since the speaker has done them the favor of speaking to their organization. If the organizations' chairpersons or presidents agree to write a letter, ask them what you can do to make it easy for them. They may ask you what type of thing you want them to say. If so, ask them to say as many good things as they can—if your presentation was engaging, entertaining, interesting, thoughtful—these are the things that other program chairpersons will want to hear about you when they are considering you as a possible speaker. Occasionally, especially if they know you well, the chairperson will tell you, "Write out what you want me to say and I'll put it in a letter." If they offer, do it and do not be bashful. Just make sure they know they can change the wording to make it their own.

❑ ASKING FOR FEEDBACK ON YOUR PRESENTATIONS

To get feedback about what people find helpful and what you could improve, whenever possible ask your audience members to fill out a brief feedback sheet. I prefer the term *feedback* to *evaluation* because the goal is not to find out how you did but how you can do better. You will never please everyone in an audience, as we have already said, but you can find out what people liked and what they would like more of. I favor a feedback sheet with open-ended questions rather than rating scales such as 1 to 5 or 1 to 10. Rating scales do not give much helpful information and they can be discouraging if you hit a bad day or a critical audience. Open-ended feedback tells you what people liked and what you may want to do differently. You can also get suggestions about other topics the audience would be interested in.

Here are the kinds of questions I do not recommend:

Rate the speaker on the following statements on a scale from 1 to 10, with 10 being outstanding and 1 being very poor:

- The speaker was well prepared and organized.

- The speaker kept my interest and attention.
- How would you rate the speaker's delivery?

Here are the kinds of questions I do recommend (see the Sample Audience Feedback Form for more examples):

- What did you like about the presentation in terms of the speaker's preparation, organization, content, interest, delivery, visual aids, handouts, etc.?
- What suggestions do you have for how the speaker could be more effective in the future in any of these areas?

Feedback forms can also be used to collect positive comments you can use in publicity for other speaking events or workshops. If someone says on your feedback form that you "kept my attention for the whole time" or "presented complicated concepts in an easy-to-understand and interesting way," can you use that quote in a brochure or flyer, as long as you do not use their name or identify them in any way? Most speakers I know would say yes, although others disagree. What is clear is that if you want to use their name with a quote, you will have to get their permission in writing. The sample feedback form that follows has a place for people to check whether you can quote them and to sign and give their name if they are willing to be quoted by name. Many more people will agree to be quoted anonymously. Either way, feedback forms are an excellent way for beginning speakers to begin gathering testimonials that can serve as recommendations.

WORKSHEET 8.1 Sample Audience Feedback Form

Your feedback is invaluable in helping me provide useful information and presentations to my audiences. I appreciate your completing this brief feedback form about the presentation/workshop.

Your name (optional) _____

What did you find most valuable and positive about the presentation/workshop? What made it helpful and/or enjoyable? (Feel free to comment on the speaker's organization, content, knowledge, delivery, audience involvement, audiovisuals, handouts, etc.)

What could I change or do differently to make the presentation more helpful, valuable, or enjoyable? Be as specific as possible.

What other topics, or aspects of today's topic, would you like to hear a presentation on?

I sometimes use statements from Audience Feedback Forms in my promotional materials. _____ If you are willing for me to use your words *without using your name*, please check here.

If you would be willing for me to *use your name* along with your comments in materials I send to other organizations who want to know more about me, please print and sign your name here (Thank You!):

Print your name _____

Sign to give permission _____

If you would like to receive occasional mailings about upcoming work-shops, presentations, or related resources, check here: _____ (Your name and address will not be shared in any way.)

Name: _____

E-mail address: _____

Mailing address: _____

CHAPTER 9

Getting Publicity for Your Presentations

YOU MAY BE TEMPTED to skip this chapter because the idea of seeking publicity for yourself turns you off, scares you, or both. If you are a therapist, you are part of a profession that has discouraged calling attention to oneself. "Start a practice and the clients will come," but do not advertise or promote yourself, has been the prevailing attitude for many years. You may be concerned about not being able to control everything the media may say about you. You may have heard stories about people being misquoted in a newspaper story and feel that you would rather have no media coverage than to be misquoted.

All these concerns are valid. I have come to realize, however, that if one has something of value to offer but no one finds out about it, the value is lost or unclaimed. I may wish that people would simply hear about me through word of mouth and call me, and many do for my therapy practice. But I make it much easier for people to learn about me and my work if I am proactive in getting the word out. I hesitate to use the term *media exposure* because exposure of the wrong kind is something we all fear. Public embarrassment feels terrible. I know that a reporter may misquote me, but I am not a person to make outlandish claims or statements, so the worst thing that has ever happened to me personally is that my name has been misspelled. I would hate to be misquoted in an embarrassing way, and it could happen, but the alternative is to keep quiet or lay low, and I am not willing to do that. You will have to do what is right for you. This chapter will describe what I think is a responsible and ethical approach to publicity. Even if your initial reaction is to shy away from seeking publicity, I encourage you to consider some of the suggestions here.

❏ WHERE TO START WITH PUBLICITY

When you give a presentation, you may speak to an audience as small as 10 or 20 people. Community organization audiences are usually not more than 100 people. You can ensure that many more people, hundreds or even thousands, read *about* you and your presentation if you take some simple but necessary steps to get media exposure or publicity for your speeches.

Most newspaper stories about local speeches and meetings come about because someone connected with the event sends a written notice, called a news release or press release, to the publication. Human interest, feature, and background stories also often stem from someone sending a news release to a newspaper editor who, based on the news release, decides to write a story. A news release can be as simple as one sentence but should seldom exceed two pages. Details about how to write a news release, including suggested formats and examples, are at the end of this chapter.

The place to begin generating media exposure is to send a news release about your presentation to all local newspapers. To do that, you will need the names and mailing or e-mail addresses or fax numbers of the newspaper sections most likely to print stories about presentations. If you read your area newspapers carefully, you will probably find sections that include upcoming meetings, presentations, or people in the news. Clip and file these as you are developing your media list. Often a note describing how to submit news items will be at the end of the column. If not, go to the newspaper's Web site and look for a link for "Contacting Us," "Where to Send News," or something similar. If you still cannot find the information, call the newspaper and ask the receptionist where you should send news about an upcoming presentation.

Ask if they have a list of addresses for sending different types of news. Most newspapers now accept, and often prefer, news releases by e-mail. Many will also accept faxes. Many newspapers now discourage sending news releases by post because e-mail is so much easier to process.

If you live in a metropolitan area, the local association of public relations professionals may publish a media directory. Check with the reference desk of your public library, the chamber of commerce, or a public relations firm (find them in the Yellow Pages) to ask if a media directory is available and how you can get a copy.

Before you send out news releases of your own, check with the organization to whom you are speaking. Sometimes clubs and organizations routinely send notices to the newspaper to list their programs. When you agree to give the speech, ask the program chairpersons how they publicize the speech and what information they need from you. They may want a brief biographical sketch and perhaps a photograph, as well as the title of your speech.

If the organization does not usually send notices to the newspaper, you can say: "I have a standard news release that I send out when I give a speech. Would you like me to go ahead and send that to the newspaper?" They will almost always be glad for you to do it.

If the club or organization has a newsletter, they will probably include an article about you and your speech in the issue prior to your presentation. Make sure you know their publication deadline and what information, including photograph, they need from you.

❏ GETTING ORGANIZED TO GET THE WORD OUT

Unless you develop a system for keeping track of media contacts and make it easy to send out news releases, you will not do it. Set up a mailing list for all your media contacts and organize it so you can send out news releases and announcements quickly and easily. A contact manager computer program like ACT or Goldmine makes it very easy, but you can also do it with Microsoft Outlook or even with a word processing program like Microsoft Word. Organize your media contacts into at least three categories—those you contact by e-mail, those you contact by fax, and those to whom you mail or hand-deliver paper copies of news releases. Keep track of what you send and when you send it, and remember to watch the newspapers to see if your notices appear. Start a clipping file of any publicity you receive. Make sure you update your media contact files regularly with any changes or additions.

❏ DEVELOPING A MEDIA KIT

If you speak regularly and often, develop a media kit (also called a press kit) about youself, your practice, your presentations or workshops, and any books or informational products you have created. The purpose of a media kit is to let an editor know about you and to provide background information that makes it easy for a reporter or editor to write a story about you. Assemble all the components of your media kit in an attractive pocket folder with your name and contact information on every piece. A basic media kit should include:

A **cover letter.** The letter should be customized for each editor and publication, if possible, and should describe why an article about you and your presentation or workshop would be of interest to their readers. Do a general version of the letter addressed to "Dear Editor or Program Chairperson," and keep a few of these general media kits with you so you can give them to someone on the spot if asked.

A **news release.** The news release in a media kit should be more than a simple announcement about your presentation and its topic. It could describe some of the key points from this or a similar presentation.

A **professional biography.** This should be written in paragraph format, not as a résumé, and be no more than two pages. Focus on the aspects of your background and credentials that make you an expert on this topic. Some media experts recommend including both a full-length bio and a condensed version (one or two paragraphs). You not only make it easier for a busy reporter or newsletter editor, but you also reduce the chances of their leaving out an aspect of your background that you want included.

A professional photograph of youself. The standard for newspapers is a black-and-white glossy (5" x 7" or 8" x 10"), but include a color version as well for Web publicity and newspapers that use color.

Marcia Yudkin (2003) suggests these other optional items that are often included in a media kit:

Previous news releases. These should highlight achievements about you or your business.

One or two previous articles. These articles should be written by you or about you, if possible. If you have been published before, that adds credibility and newsworthiness for an editor.

Other marketing or publicity material. Include a practice brochure or workshop flyer if you have one.

A list of talking points. What are the interesting key points or questions about your topic that an editor might use as points in a story. Make it easy for a reporter or editor to find something to write about you.

A tip sheet. This can be a list of short tips, one paragraph each, related to your presentation topic, such as "10 Ways to Destress the Holidays" or "7 Steps to Becoming a Better Listener." Editors love numbered lists of brief, pithy tips because they can pick two or three to fit the space they have available for their story.

A list of clients. This would be appropriate for a business coach, for example, but obviously not for personal coaches or psychotherapists.

A list of organizations where you have spoken or media you have appeared in. As your speaking engagements expand beyond the local Kiwanis and Rotary to include associations and corporations, you may want to include them here. If you appear on radio or television programs or are published in periodicals, you can include a listing of the best.

Quotations about you and your work. Include these if you have quotations or testimonials about you by people whose names or positions would add credibility in the eyes of an editor. This can carry a heading such as "What Others Are Saying about [Your Name].

❏ PUBLICIZING BEYOND THE LOCAL NEWSPAPER

Local newspaper listings for meetings and people in the news are a good place to start with publicizing your presentations, but you should not stop there. Other local media to send your news releases to include:

- Features or specialty editors or columnists in the local newspapers. For coaches and therapists, these might include editors of the business, health, or lifestyles sections.
- Hosts for local talk radio programs.
- Hosts for local television programs that use local guests or television reporters that focus on business-, health-, or lifestyle-related stories.
- Editors of area business newspapers. Most communities of 500,000 or more have a weekly business journal that carries a "people in the news" section as well as features about local businesses.
- Editors of area university newspapers. This will be most appropriate if you or your presentation are related to the university, or if the topic relates to student or faculty issues.

Why send your news releases to all these media? Even though many of them do not carry listings of meetings and presentations, editors and reporters are always looking for interesting stories and knowledgeable experts to interview. You cannot know whether a television reporter has been thinking about doing a story on stress in the workplace or communication strategies for couples. If your news release crosses a newspaper desk or computer screen at the right time, you may be the person a reporter calls when she is looking for an expert.

Although your initial news releases may be simple announcements of presentations, the more exposure you get in the media, the more likely you will be invited to speak. You can take advantage of this synergy by sending news releases on other occasions besides presentations or workshops. In addition to presentations, you can send news releases to announce:

- Receiving an award, recognition, or other distinction
- Achieving a new certification
- Moving and expanding your office
- Adding a staff member or associate
- Getting a new major customer or contract (make sure you have permission of the customer)
- Announcing the results of a research project or survey
- Offering a new or significantly modified service or product
- Being named an officer or board member of a professional association
- Holding an open house at your business
- Donating your services in a unique way to the community

One of the most effective news releases is one in which you, as a professional, comment with recommendations on a current news event or phenomenon. After 9/11, therapists were frequently interviewed in the media about ways to deal with the aftereffects of the terrorism. Any news that makes local or national headlines can be the basis for offering observations and suggestions through a news release. Here are some news events from the past that therapists or coaches could comment on:

- School violence
- Infidelity by a well-known leader
- Families disrupted by war
- Layoffs and unemployment

- Unethical behavior in the workplace
- Changing family, work, and societal patterns (dual career, women in the military, stay-at-home dads, children raised by grandparents, generational changes or differences, changing attitudes toward money, changing roles of men and women, changing sexual attitudes, etc.). The change you comment on does not need to be "news" as long as it is a phenomenon that would be recognized. Faith Popcorn created a bestselling book and successful speaking career by naming and commenting on changing societal patterns such as "cocooning," the tendency of people to go out less to shop and socialize.
- News stories about research findings related to stress, sleep, family life, mental or physical health, illnesses, psychotherapy and other treatments, schools, work, jobs, and so on.
- Seasonal and holiday events—end of school, back to school, starting college, holiday stress, New Year's (resolutions, making changes), winter blues, time change, a major storm that disrupts normal life, a snowstorm that could cause cabin fever, to name a few. Special days and months designated to focus on a topic can also be good reasons for a story. Examples include National Mental Health Month and National Anxiety Awareness Week. *Chase's Calendar of Events,* available in most public library reference collections, is a "day-by-day directory to special days, weeks and months as well as holidays, historical anniversaries and fairs and festivals."

When a story breaks that has a connection to your area of expertise, put together a quick news release and send it by e-mail or fax to an editor you know at the local newspaper. Tell them you would be glad to provide background information if they are interested. Since it is a time-sensitive topic, you may decide to follow up by phone to see if they are interested in doing a story on the topic. You certainly do not want to be a pest, but a phone call can make sure they do not completely overlook your idea in the avalanche of news releases they receive.

If you have been speaking for a while and have a message that you think would interest media beyond your immediate area, how can you get wider coverage? If you get a feature story published in a local newspaper, it may be picked up by a national wire service and published in other newspapers. The first you know about it may be a letter or phone call from another part of the country where someone has read the story.

You can also write a new release and make it available to media all over the world using services available through the Internet. One such free basic service is available through prnewswire.com, although you can increase your exposure by paying for premium service.

❏ PITCHING A STORY

You can hope an editor reads one of your news releases and decides to do a story on your topic. Or you can take the initiative to suggest or "pitch" a story to the media. The process of pitching a story is fairly simple. Identify a topic idea and a slant that you think would make a good story. Choose one reporter or editor whose coverage includes stories of this type and make your proposal to one editor only. They do not want to pick up a neighboring newspaper and discover a similar story that you also offered to them. Write a letter to the reporter or editor, describing the idea in a brief and engaging way. Get to the point quickly and lead with an attention-getting statement or question (called a "hook" because you want to hook their attention). Focus on what about the story makes it newsworthy and why it would interest and benefit their readers. Forget how it may benefit you. If an editor catches even a whiff of self-promotion, you will strike out with your own pitch. You are suggesting that the editor let you write the story or assign a writer to do the story, presumably using you as a resource.

A story pitch, unless you have an ongoing relationship with an editor, should be mailed or hand-delivered. E-mail, especially from an unfamiliar source, can be easily overlooked by a busy editor. In your pitch letter, you should include day and evening phone numbers as well as an e-mail address that you check frequently. The editor may send you a note saying, "Thanks, but no thanks." If so, pitch it to someone else. The editor may contact you and suggest a variation on your story idea or suggest an entirely different story. If you are asked to write the story, you will have to decide if you want to use the suggested approach. You can certainly do some negotiating based on your own knowledge and experience. If the new story idea really is not a good fit for you, say so, but make it clear that you would be interested in doing another story sometime in the future. Once you have made a positive contact with an editor, you will have an easier time promoting story ideas in the future.

If you do not hear from the editor within a few days, call. Be succinct in explaining that you sent a story proposal a few days before, on *[give date]*, and you were calling to make sure it was received. If the editor did not receive it or does not remember it, tell him you will send it again. Give the editor the bullet points of the idea and two sentences about why you are the person to write it or be interviewed about it. If the editor says, "No, not interested," say you may have other story ideas to propose in the future and ask if you could send one from time to time. The editor will almost surely say yes and you have opened a door and a relationship.

❏ CULTIVATING RELATIONSHIPS WITH THE MEDIA

If you want to improve the chances of your news releases getting media attention, get to know some of the reporters and editors in your area. If they recognize your name, they are more likely to look at what you send them. If they know you to be a thoughtful and articulate authority on certain topics, they will contact you when they are writing a story related to your expertise.

How do you cultivate relationships with reporters and editors? Send them well-written news releases periodically, following the protocol outlined here and on their publication's web site. If you see reporters' stories that you think are well done, send the reporters e-mails telling them you liked them, and why. As you identify writers who publish stories on topics related to your expertise, send them a media kit to introduce yourself, making sure you use a personalized cover letter to make the connection between your area of experience and their stories. Tell them that you would be glad to serve as a resource on certain topics (and name the topics). Make sure they have all your phone numbers and e-mail address, and return their calls or e-mails immediately—they may have a short deadline.

If you send your news release to more than one editor or department, add a note to them saying, for example: "I sent a copy of this release to 'People in the News' but thought you might be interested in the human interest side of this topic."

❏ WRITING A NEWS RELEASE

Marcia Yudkin (2003) describes how to write a news release in six simple steps:[*]

Step One: Write a Headline with a News Angle

If the news release is about a presentation you will give, the "news angle" for your headline may be that you are speaking on a particular topic: BUSINESS COACH TO SPEAK ON WORKPLACE ETIQUETTE. If you take a position or express a point of view, it will be more interesting in terms of news: BUSINESS COACH SAYS POOR WORKPLACE ETIQUETTE COSTS COMPANIES MILLIONS.

Avoid headlines that are too general. For example, BUSINESS COACH TO GIVE PRESENTATION does not give enough information to catch an editor's interest.

Step Two: Present the Basic Information about the Story in the First Paragraph

This is where you work in the Who, What, Where, When, Why, and How. If the news release is a simple announcement of your presentation, you would give information about your topic and the organization you are speaking to as well as where and when the meeting will be held.

---

[*] From *Six Steps to Free Publicity*, Revised Edition, by Marcia Yudkin, Career Press, 2003. Used with premission.

Reece A. Franklin (1996) suggests you make sure you answer these questions in your news release:*

Who are you, your service, or your client?
What is the event, or the subject of your story?
Where is the event being held?
When is the event being held?
Why is it unique or different?
How does it work or how can someone get more information?

If you are taking a position, you would state the basics of your position and then say you will be giving a presentation on the topic to such and such organization, and give the date, time, and place.

Step Three: Use a Lively Quote that Elaborates on the Facts of the Story for the Next Paragraph

Since this news release is about your presentation, quote yourself in relation to your topic. A benefit-based quote can be especially good, such as what people who attend the workshop will learn.

For example: "All the etiquette you really need to know you can learn in an hour," business coach Julia Barrett says. She will demonstrate quick and entertaining ways to teach the basic rules of etiquettes in her presentation. "Etiquette doesn't have to be boring. It can be fun, and it can certainly make social interactions go more smoothly," she said.

Do not simply restate the topic in the quote without adding anything; the editor will delete the quote if you do. In the example above, you would not say: "This is a presentation on business etiquette," says business Coach Julia Barrett. "Etiquette is important," she says, "and that's why we all need to learn it." The quote restates the obvious.

Step Four: Elaborate Further on the Basic Facts in the Third Paragraph

In this paragraph you may give a brief statement about you or about the organization you will be speaking to. You may also give further evidence or elaboration for the position you have taken.

---

* From *A Consultant's Guide to Publicity* by Reece A. Franklin. ©Copyright 1996. Reprinted by permission of JohnWiley & Sons, Inc.

Step Five: End with the Any Other Needed Details

If there are any contact details for the presentation, include them at the end.

Step Six: Send It Out

Be sure to include all the information needed for the story, especially date, time, and location. Otherwise, an editor will throw out your release. They are too busy to call you for the missing details.

Make sure you write the story as news, not as an advertisement. Avoid superlative adjectives such as "outstanding," "leading," or "well-known," since these are descriptions of opinion, not fact. Ask yourself whether your competition would take issue with anything you say about yourself in your news release. If so, is it factual? If not, take it out.

Before you can send out your release, you need to know one last detail—how to format the news release.

❑ FORMATTING A NEWS RELEASE

At the top center of the page, in larger type, are the words *News Release* or *News*.

Below that, usually on the left, is *Contact* information, which is the name, phone numbers, and e-mail address of the person the editor could call to get more information. These should include an evening phone number since newspaper staff often work into the evening. A mailing address is usually included.

Opposite the contact information on the right, you should put the date you are sending the release and the phrase: FOR IMMEDIATE RELEASE. Some news announcements are sent out in advance with a release date, so this tells the editor that this news can be announced immediately.

The headline for the story should be centered in all caps. For example: "PSYCHOLOGIST WILL SPEAK ON TEENAGE DEPRES-SION." This isn't exciting, but it tells the editor at a glance what the story is about. Print the headline in a bold font, a size or two larger than the story itself.

Under the main headline, you can add a subhead, sometimes called a *deck* or *deck-head,* that summarizes a main point of the story in one sentence to create more interest among editors skimming news releases. Do not simply rephrase the main headline and keep the subhead to no more than 14 words. The subhead is usually a couple fonts smaller than the headline and may use initial caps (title case). The subhead for the headline above might be: "Speaker Says Education and Aggressive Treatment Can Save Hundreds of Lives."

The story itself is written in normal text (not all caps), double-spaced, using the "inverted pyramid" format of standard journalism. In the "inverted pyramid," the most essential and basic information comes first, including information about Who, What, Where, When, Why, and How.

If the news release goes to a second page, do not divide a paragraph between the two pages. Also, at the bottom center of the first page, put the word *"more."* The reason for these rules is that pages can get separated on editors' desks. The pages should *not* be stapled.

At the end of the story, put either "# # #" or "-30-" (without the quotes) which are journalists' symbols for "The End." This tells them there are no more pages.

If possible, include a glossy black-and-white photograph of yourself with the news release. This will increase your chances of the item being printed and gives you better exposure. Put identifying information (your name, address, and phone number) on a sheet of paper taped to the back of the photograph (not a Post-it note because it can fall off too easily). In most cases, the newspaper will not return the photograph, but they will often keep it on file and use it again.

❏ SAMPLE BASIC NEWS RELEASES

News Release 9.1

For Immediate Release
[Current date and year]
Contact: Joseph Masterson, Ph.D.
                  555 Your Street
                  Your City, NY [ZIP]
                  (555) 555-5555 (day)
                  (555) 555-5556 (evening)

PSYCHOLOGIST WILL SPEAK TO NURSES' ASSOCIATION ON SLEEP PROBLEMS AND THEIR TREATMENT

Speaker Says Loss of Sleep Is Serious But Treatable Epidemic

Your City, NY: Dr. Joseph Masterson will speak on "Methods for Treating Health-Related Sleep Problems" at the Triangle Nurses' Association monthly meeting next Friday, September 30, at 7:30 p.m., at the Park Doubletree Inn. The meeting is open to the public.

Dr. Masterson is a psychologist in private practice specializing in counseling people with chronic illness and health-related problems.

"Health professionals can learn new ways to help their patients based on the latest sleep research," Dr. Masterson said. "Sleep problems are often a source of unnecessary suffering for patients with chronic illnesses. Many new treatments are available that we didn't have five years ago," he said.

For information about the meeting, call (555) 555-5559.

# # #

❏ ANOTHER SAMPLE NEWS RELEASE

News Release 9.2

For Immediate Release
[Current date and year]
Contact: Joseph Masterson, Ph.D.
                555 Your Street
                Your City, NY [ZIP]
                (555) 555-5555 (day)
                (555) 555-5556 (evening)

PSYCHOLOGIST SAYS TURNING OFF TV CAN IMPROVE SLEEP

Report Offers Practical Tips for Overcoming Insomnia

Your City, NY: People who have trouble falling asleep might try turning off the TV and dimming the lights for at least half an hour before going to bed. That's just one recommendation given by Dr. Joseph Masterson, a psychologist who specializes in counseling people with health-related problems.

"Many people go to bed right after being stimulated by disturbing newscasts or by dramatic police or medical programs and they can't sleep. TV can be as stimulating as a cup of coffee," Dr. Masterson says. He made his comments Friday at a workshop for hospice and home health nurses.

He recommends that people turn off the TV and dim the lights for thirty to sixty minutes before going to bed. "Bright lights also stimulate wakefulness. By dimming the lights, we give our brains the signal that it's time to get ready for sleep," he says. People may not see the results the first night, he says, but he's found it helps with many of the clients he counsels.

Readers may get a free copy of Dr. Masterson's report titled "12 Tips for Getting More Restful Sleep" at his Web site (www.drmastersonexample.com) or by sending a self-addressed stamped (37 cents postage) business-size envelope to: Joseph Masterson, Ph.D., 555 Your Street, Your City, NY ZIP.

# # #

CHAPTER 10

Designing and Delivering Workshops, Seminars, and Training

WHEN YOU GIVE PRESENTATIONS to community, business, or professional groups, it will not be long before someone asks you if you offer workshops or if you are available to do training. If you are already doing workshops and seminars, you will probably be asked if you ever do speeches. Each is a natural complement and outgrowth of the other. In this chapter we will discuss the types of workshops and seminars that therapists and coaches conduct, and what you need to know to create and conduct outstanding workshops.

What are the differences among workshops, seminars, and training? Workshops and seminars are both educational in nature, with workshops usually focused on teaching and learning skills and seminars more often focused on content rather than skills. Workshops usually include more audience-participation activities and hands-on experience than seminars. Workshops and seminars typically run from 2 hours to 2 days, although they can be as short as 45 minutes and as long as a week. *Training* is a broad term used to describe any education of employees in skills or processes (how to do things). *Training* may also refer to ongoing education of employees, whereas workshops and seminars usually describe training *events* lasting no more than a few days at most. Since the information you need to successfully plan and implement any of these events is basically the same, I will use the terms interchangeably unless I specify otherwise.

Until recently, workshops always implied a group of people gathering in a single location for the event. Technology now makes it possible for people all over the world to participate in educational events by telephone, videoconferencing, or interactive Internet connections. Telephone seminars are usually called teleclasses or teleconferences. We will talk about conducting teleclasses in a separate section later in the chapter.

❏ DECIDING WHETHER TO DO A WORKSHOP

Workshops can be divided into two main categories: (a) those sponsored by an organization other than your own, and (b) those you design and produce on your own.

If someone asks you to conduct a workshop or you consider submitting a proposal to lead a workshop for a company or a conference, answer the following questions about a possible workshop sponsored by someone else *before* you commit yourself:

1. Do you have the experience and knowledge to lead a workshop on this topic? If not, can you reasonably develop the expertise needed to lead an effective workshop on this topic? Do the topic and focus they are proposing fit with your interests and planned direction for your practice? What alternate topic would you propose for this workshop?

When first starting out to do public speaking, many therapists and coaches are so happy to be invited that they are willing to develop a workshop on almost any reasonable topic. What they soon discover is that developing workshops takes *a lot of time*. Even if you are being paid well for the workshop, it may not be worth the time and effort if the topic and content are ones you will never use again, either because the topic is highly specialized or the topic is not one that fits with your main professional focus.

If the topic is not one you want to do, find out how committed the organization is to the particular topic. Find out what they want to accomplish with the workshop. I have found that often the original stated topic is only an idea that someone suggested, and that they are delighted when you propose something that they like even better. If their topic is not a good fit for you, and your suggested alternatives do not fit for them, be prepared to decline the invitation, making it clear that you hope they will consider you again in the future. Saying no is not easy for many of us, but it is much easier than spending days developing a workshop that you regret agreeing to do.

2.   How much time will it take to design and lead the workshop? What materials would be needed for this workshop? How many of these materials are already available and what would need to be created? Will you be able to use the workshop content again with others in this organization or other organizations? Do you have the time and are you willing to commit the time to this project?

If you have not created many workshops, you may find it difficult to estimate the time you will need. Even if you know the topic well, developing handouts and exercises can easily take an hour or more for every hour of the workshop itself. If you have to research and develop the content also, you need to at least double or triple that estimate. Be sure to allow time for consulting with the sponsor/client about their needs, objectives, and expectations. The more directly involved the sponsor is in helping design the event, the more time you will need to develop the workshop.

If the workshop topic and design are ones you will be able to use again, especially if you can use them several times, you may be willing to invest more time in developing the workshop for this audience.

Repeating a workshop, even with revisions and customizing, takes much less development time after the first time.

3.   Who will the audience be? Do you enjoy working and work well with this type of audience? Will the audience members be at similar levels in terms of what they know and how they will use the workshop content? If not, how could you deal with those different levels? Will the audience members choose to attend or be required to attend?

You may be able to work well with a wide variety of people, but you probably work better with some types of audiences than others. If you will have difficulty developing rapport with the intended audience, think hard before agreeing to do the workshop. Listen to your gut, but also ask lots of questions about who the audience will be and what they will want from the workshop. Having an audience at very different levels of experience (professionals and consumers in the same workshop, for example) can be challenging. When participants are expected or required to attend as part of their job or a court order, for example, you have an even bigger challenge. None of these are reasons not to do the workshop, but they are factors to consider in deciding whether you want to take on the challenge.

4.   What are the objectives and expectations of the sponsoring organization and of the expected audience? Are the objectives and expectations of both groups clear, realistic, and compatible?

Many times the sponsoring organizations do not know what their objectives and expectations are. They just want to put on a workshop. Part of your job is to help them get clearer about what they want and why. Why are they planning to do this workshop now? What do they hope will happen as a result of this workshop? What problems do they hope it will address and how? What would a successful workshop look like, and how would they know that it was successful? Listen closely to what they say, and what you know about the audience. Sometimes, organizations have a serious problem and they are looking for a silver bullet or easy answer. They may hope a workshop will solve the problem or shape people up. You want to make sure that the expectations are clear and attainable if you are going to do the workshop.

5.   Does the sponsoring organization have the staffing, organizational skills, and commitment to do their part in organizing the logistics for the workshop? What staff support will they provide for setting up the room, registering participants as they arrive, taking care of meals, and so on?

The logistics of organizing a workshop require attention to detail and significant time. For workshops sponsored by someone else, your role, unless you agree otherwise, is to design and lead the workshop, but not to handle the logistics. For workshops sponsored by nonprofit organizations, you may be asked if you can handle many of the logistics. You will want to decide how the room should be arranged, but you may be expected to get involved in the physical arrangements, including carrying tables and chairs from one room to another. "Just let people sign in as they arrive" can mean there is no one available to answer questions about payment or lost registrations. These kinds of activities may interfere with your being able to lead the workshop, so make sure from the beginning that you will have adequate help with the logistics.

6.   What fee would you need to receive for developing and presenting this workshop? What fee are they offering? What are the terms of the contract concerning payment, cancellation of the workshop by the sponsor or by you, expenses, and other related matters?

You have already thought about how much time it would take. How much would you charge for this amount of time? Usually workshop fees are expected to cover developing the workshop as well as leading it. Handouts and materials are sometimes included in the fee, but you need to be clear about this. Expenses are usually reimbursed separately. Even if you are using materials you have already created, you will need to customize them for this workshop, and thus expenses will be involved.

Sometimes an organization that approaches you to lead a workshop will tell you up front how much they expect to pay. More often than not, they will ask you how much you would charge to do the workshop. Before you state your fee, find out as much as you can about their plans by getting answers to the questions you have just read about as well as the following:

How many people will attend?
How long will the workshop last?
Will people pay to attend? If so, how much will the registration cost?
Where will the event be held?
What audiovisual equipment will be needed and who will provide it?
Will materials be included in the fee or budgeted separately?
Will travel, meals, and lodging, if any, be reimbursed separately?
What do they have budgeted for the workshop?

Before you start designing the workshop, you should have a signed contract or letter of agreement spelling out all the terms.

An important point to clarify in writing is what happens if you or the organization has to cancel. Most scheduled workshops take place as planned, but organizations sometimes cancel because of low registration, budget cuts, or changes in the organization. Occasionally, an organization wants you to hold multiple dates while they decide which one will work. You may think the organization has committed to doing the workshop, when they have only "penciled it in" as a possibility. To protect yourself as a workshop leader, seek a cutoff date beyond which the organization will be responsible for some or all of your fee if they cancel. This way, if they cancel after you have designed and prepared for the workshop, you will receive payment. You may also have turned away other business to hold the date for the organization's workshop. Many workshop leaders ask for a deposit of one third or one half of the workshop fee when the contract is signed, with the remainder of the fee due at the conclusion of the workshop. If the event is canceled because of bad weather, you may have a provision for rescheduling without a penalty to the organization.

In case *you* have to cancel because of illness, family emergency, or a travel snafu, seek a provision for rescheduling the workshop without a penalty to you. If you are coleading the workshop, the coleader may be able to go on without you, but this should be spelled out in the contract.

Up to now, we have been discussing workshops, seminars, and training done in conjunction with another organization. The other main category of workshops are those you put on yourself.

❏ STARTING TO PUT ON YOUR OWN WORKSHOP

Before you are ready to plan and produce your own workshop, give some presentations and lead workshops in conjunction with organizations. Learn the basics of what works with various kinds of audiences and what your own strengths and challenges are as a leader and presenter. Improve your skill and confidence as a workshop leader before you consider putting on your own workshop.

Why would you want to produce your own workshop? The most common reasons are:

- You want to call the shots about the content and design of the workshop. When you do a workshop through or for another organization, they usually have a say in what you cover and how you design it. If you do your own, as long as you do something that works for your audience, you can do it your way.

- You want to do a topic or take an approach that does not fit the interests of the organizations you know. If you have an idea for a workshop that is outside the mainstream, you may not find an organization that wants to offer it.

- Workshops sponsored by you and your business can be an excellent way to get exposure and build a reputation in a geographical area or in a specialty. If you have a unique approach or exceptional experience with certain techniques, you may choose to offer training programs or a certification process. A training program usually consists of a series of workshops or classes, sometimes with beginning to advanced levels, over the course of a year or more.

- You want to do workshops as an income source. You want to make money from doing them. Many therapists and coaches use workshops and training as one of their income streams, and some do very well with them.

Because of the time, effort, and money required to publicize a workshop that you offer on your own, you would do best to work with workshops sponsored by others first, unless you meet the following:

- You already have a sizeable mailing list and can send out mailings (or have someone send out mailings *for* you) fairly easily.

- You are well connected and/or well known in the community so that your leadership will make the workshop appealing to a certain number of people.

- You are presenting the workshop on a topic that is interesting and topical enough in itself to generate easy publicity and interest.

- You already have a space for the workshop either in your own office or in a convenient facility you can borrow or rent inexpensively.

- You can collaborate with one or more colleagues to pool your mailing lists and your publicity efforts.

- You will be happy charging a modest fee for the workshop (or no fee at all) and you will not lose much money if the workshop gets only a small enrollment or is canceled because of low enrollment or bad weather.

If you meet most of the criteria just listed or have had some experience doing workshops through other organizations, you may want to try your hand at producing your own workshop.

A simple way is to start by offering a free evening presentation on a topic related to your practice. If you can hold the meeting at your office, you get exposure for your location in the publicity and with the participants. Also, the people who attend have shown that they find your office location accessible. If you use a space on the other side of town, you may attract people who might find it less convenient to travel to your office. Some therapists offer a regular series of programs at their offices, rotating the leadership among the other therapists in their group. The advantages of this approach are that it can usually generate some regular publicity and establish you as an expert on the topics presented. The disadvantage is that you will probably reach a fairly small number of people, including some people who are current clients.

If you do not have space at your office (or your office is in your home), you may be able to use a library, church, or bank community room at no charge, as long as the workshop is free. Using libraries or church facilities can have the advantage of increasing exposure since these organizations may publicize the event among their own constituents, if you provide them with flyers and an article for their newsletter.

Before you start any detailed planning and designing, decide on your general purpose for holding a workshop. If your purpose is to get exposure and possibly attract new clients or referrals, you can probably accomplish that with short workshops of $1^1/_2$ to 3 hours. These workshops can range in cost from free to $50 per session. A model that some people have used successfully is to offer a 4- to 8-week workshop series with people paying for the series or having the option of paying only for those they choose to attend. A modest fee of $10 or $15 per evening may cover your expenses.

If your purpose is to develop an income stream from your workshops, you can offer many short evening workshops so that your mailing and publicity costs are divided among several events that you publicize at once. If you have a space to hold these workshops and do not have to rent space each time, this approach can work as an income source. The limitations of evening workshops as a source of income are that many people will resist paying more than $35 or $40 for an evening workshop or traveling more than 30 or 40 minutes each way, thus limiting both the amount you can earn and the numbers you can attract.

One- or two-day workshops are more viable as a source of income for several reasons:

- People expect to pay much more for a one- or two-day workshop than for an evening event. The registration fee can be anywhere between $75 and $195 per day for a typical mental health or coaching workshop, depending on the topic, the leader, the audience, and the geographical area. For some medical and business workshops, the fees may range much higher.
- The cost of marketing, providing meeting facilities, and producing handouts typically takes a smaller percentage of the income with a longer workshop than with a shorter one.
- A daylong workshop is perceived as having much more value than a short evening workshop.
- People employed by an agency, hospital, or business generally prefer to attend professional workshops during working hours than during the evening when it would take away from personal time.
- People are willing to travel farther for a daylong workshop than for an evening event, thus significantly increasing the number of possible attendees.
- People are likely to purchase more collateral materials such as books, CDs, tapes, and videos at a longer event, partly because

they have more time to browse, but also because they have a higher interest and commitment to the topic as demonstrated by their attending the longer workshop.

Most people who want to produce their own workshop think that their main task is to design and lead the workshop. In truth, a more critical task is *marketing* the workshop. If you do not get enough people for your workshop, you will not have the opportunity to lead it or your expenses will cost more than your revenue. If you are going to be successful in producing your own workshop, think about the marketing of your workshop from the beginning.

Start by deciding on an appealing topic and an audience whom you can reach easily with your marketing and who will be interested in a workshop on that topic. The topic and the audience are closely linked. You cannot decide on a good topic without deciding on the audience, and you cannot choose an audience without deciding the topic of the workshop.

After you have identified an audience and a possible topic, talk with several people who are representative of your intended audience to find out what would make a workshop on that topic most appealing and helpful to them. If the workshop is for therapists, talk with therapists. If the workshop is for independent professionals, talk with independent professionals like those you would expect to attend. Ask them whether and what about the topic appeals to them, what are the challenges they have in relation to the topic, what they want to learn more about, what would not be particularly interesting to them, and so on. You will get a reading about whether the topic sounds like a good one for your audience. You will also get ideas for slanting the topic, designing the workshop, and writing effective descriptions for your advertising and publicity.

The key that many people overlook in their planning is the importance of choosing an audience they can easily reach with their marketing. While advertisements, calendar listings, and word of mouth can influence people to sign up for a workshop, most people sign up for workshops because they receive a flyer or brochure about it. The flyer may be printed or electronic, with people increasingly directed to Web sites for the details and registration forms for workshops.

Another factor that many overlook is that even when a well-targeted audience receives well-designed flyers about a workshop that would be relevant to them, only 1% to 2% of the people sign up for the workshop. Robert Bly (2001) says that the sign-up rate for seminar mailings ranges between 0.25% and 3%, with the typical rate being between 0.5% and 1%. That means you will need to send out notices to at least 100 times as many people as you want to sign up. So if you want to get 20 people to sign up for your workshop, you need to mail flyers to at least 2,000 people who would be likely participants for such a workshop. Of course, the rate of registration may be higher if you are well known, the topic is timely, the workshop provides required continuing education credit, no one else is offering training on this topic, and the workshop does not conflict with other popular events. But the return may be much less than 1% if another workshop was recently offered on a similar topic, if the flyer is not appealing, if the mailing arrives too early or too late, or a host of other factors I will try to help you avoid.

To be successful in getting people to sign up for the workshop, you must target groups you can contact easily and inexpensively. If you already have a large mailing list of people who know you and your work and who would be interested in workshops you would offer, you may be able to fill your workshops easily. If you do not have your own mailing list, your other options are to get other organizations to let you use their mailing lists (or do a mailing on your behalf), to compile a mailing list from phone directories and other lists you can find, or to rent mailing lists from a list brokerage company.

If you are planning a small workshop and only need a few people to make it worthwhile, you may be able to send flyers to organizations and colleagues you know, asking them to pass the flyers on to others who might be interested. You should do this no matter what else you do. If you have a good reputation or choose a hot topic, this may be enough.

You may also be able to arrange for some organizations to do a mailing to their members on your behalf. Some therapist and business organizations will supply, for a fee, a set of mailing labels of their members. For an additional fee, you may be able to have their administrative staff put the labels on your flyers and mail them. With growing concerns about privacy, fewer organizations are willing to do this than in the past, but it may be an option to explore.

If you are on a tight budget, you may be tempted to make your own mailing lists from membership directories or Yellow Page listings. Before using membership directories to create a list, make sure you will not be violating the membership rules by using the list for commercial purposes. You do not want your exciting workshop project to get started under a cloud. Before you laboriously transcribe Yellow Page listings into your computer, or pay someone to do it for you, contact list brokers to see what lists are available and how much they would cost. You may find commercial lists more economical.

❑ MAILING LISTS, LIST BROKERS, AND MAILING SERVICES

Mailing list brokers compile mailing lists from various sources such as the telephone directories, licensing board lists, conference registration lists, journal subscription lists, book purchasers, and so on. They enter their lists into computer databases so they can sort the names by profession, ZIP code, area code, city or town, county, and the like. List brokers then rent the lists to people or organizations for their mailings. Most brokers can supply the names and addresses on various styles of mailing labels (peel-off or gummed) or in a database that you can use to address labels or envelopes. You rent the list rather than buy it with the restriction that you are usually only allowed to make one mailing to the list for the fee that you pay. List brokers usually monitor list use by tracking certain names on the rented list so they will know if you use the list again.

Mailing lists are usually priced per 1,000 names. Many list brokers have a 5,000-name minimum, while others have a $250 minimum order and charge a higher per 1,000 rate for fewer than 5,000 names.

If you wanted to do a mailing to psychologists, clinical social workers, and marriage and family therapists in your ZIP code or telephone area code, a list broker could tell you how many of each profession are in their database. The list broker might also suggest other related lists such as mental health centers, psychiatrists, or clinical nurse specialists (psychiatric nurses).

Unless you want to peel and stick 2,000 labels on flyers, as well as the closures that keep the flyer from unfolding, you may want to look into using a mailing service (sometimes called a letter shop). A mailing service is a business that puts together mailings for businesses and organizations. Depending on the service, they may also offer layout and printing services as well. They usually work closely with list brokers and know which list brokers are the best to work with. Mailing services also know the ins and outs of mailing regulations, mailing rates, how to save money on postage, how long each type of mail takes, and so on. They can advise you on less expensive alternatives to first-class mail. They have specialized equipment that can do in an hour what would take a day or more to do by hand. Ask around and find a mailing service that works with small mailings. Tell them what you are planning to do and ask them everything you need to know. My local favorite, Always Remembered Mailing Service, is a wealth of information and expertise. They can usually do a mailing less expensively, and always with less hassle, than I can do myself. Check your local Yellow Pages under "Mailing Services" and also under "Mailing Lists."

❏ DEVELOPING YOUR OWN MAILING LIST

No matter what kind of speaking or workshops you expect to do, start developing your own mailing list now. Even if all you do is record names and addresses in a notebook, start doing it. If possible, learn to use one of the contact management software programs such as ACT or Goldmine, or use the Contacts section of Microsoft Outlook. Because e-mail is becoming such a common method of written communication, the most important information for your mailing list may be people's names and e-mail addresses. You can set up your own electronic mailing list through a number of online services, including Yahoogroups.com, which is free. Other online services and software make it relatively inexpensive and easy to set up your own e-zine or electronic newsletter. You may only use the electronic list to send out notices of workshops and presentations or to get feedback on ideas for seminars. But if you want to do seminars and workshops in the future, your mailing list can become one of the most valuable tools for getting the word out.

I recently received an e-mail from a coach I know, announcing that she would be reading from her new book on an upcoming Sunday afternoon. I wanted to go in support of her and to see what the event would be like. There were at least 50 people there, almost all of whom came because she had kept in touch with them through her e-mail list. Her reading was free, but she probably sold books to most of the people who attended.

❏ WHAT TO INCLUDE IN YOUR SEMINAR FLYER

Your workshop or seminar flyer must be more than a fact sheet. It should make interested readers want to attend because of the description of what they would learn. The description of the workshop should include a list of bullet points stating the benefits participants will get by attending. These are often stated to include a bit of mystery and intrigue by using phrases such as:

Participants will learn:

- 4 essential steps necessary for . . .
- 3 overlooked keys to . . .
- 5 best methods for . . .
- The 10 mistakes that most beginners make in . . . and how to avoid them.

You also need to make sure you include all the information that prospective participants may want to know. Robert Bly recommends that every seminar mailing include the following:

1. The title of the program.
2. A description of the program.

3. The benefits the reader will get if registering for the program.
4. A list of bulleted items describing the specific things the reader will learn in the seminar. The more complete the list is, the better.
5. Testimonials from others who have taken the seminar (if available).
6. Instructor's biography and qualifications to lead the seminar.
7. Date and hours of the seminar.
8. Name of hotel or meeting facility, address, and location.
9. Fee.
10. Registration coupon and instructions on how to register.
11. Cancellation policy.
12. Food arrangements (lunch provided? coffee? tea?).
13. Phone numbers to call in case the reader has questions.
14. Early registration discount, if any, for registration by a certain date.

An e-mail address and web site where they can get more information are also essential.

If you are offering a workshop for therapists, it pays to get approved to offer continuing education credits for the different categories of therapists: psychologists, clinical social workers, licensed professional counselors, and so on. Check with the licensing organizations in your state for the requirements.

❏ DECIDING WHEN AND WHERE TO HOLD YOUR WORKSHOP

In addition to deciding on the topic and the audience for your workshop, you will also need to find a place to hold it and decide on a date for it. These two decisions must be made in tandem since you usually cannot know if a space is available unless you choose a date, and you cannot choose a date unless you know you have a place to hold the workshop.

One approach is to pick two or three possible dates and double-check the calendar to make sure they do not conflict with religious or secular holidays or major sporting events. If you hope to attract university faculty, staff, or students, make sure your planned dates do not fall during final exams or a vacation break for local colleges and universities.

Be sure you have enough lead time to plan and publicize your workshop. For a daylong workshop, you should have flyers in people's hands at least 8 weeks before the event. That means you will need to have the flyer written, designed, and printed, and have your mailing lists ready to go at least 10 weeks before the event. Everything always takes longer than you expect. For your first daylong workshop you should probably start planning 6 months in advance, with 4 months as an absolute minimum. If you are planning an evening event of 2 or 3 hours, you can probably do it with considerably less lead time, probably as little as 2 months.

For small evening workshops, you may be able to use your office if you have a large enough space. The advantage of using your own office space, if you see clients at your office, is that participants get a sense of what it would be like to come see you as a client. The main disadvantage to using your own space is that you may not be able to accommodate as many people as you could elsewhere. Other possible spaces for evening workshops include conference or training rooms of nearby businesses or nonprofit organizations, community rooms of a bank or library, church or synagogue meeting rooms, school meeting rooms, condominium clubhouses, college and university facilities, arts centers, community theaters, and hotel, club, and restaurant meeting rooms. If you are offering a free workshop as an outreach to the community or to let people know about your services, you will have more options than if you are charging for the workshop, since community rooms and religious organizations may have restrictions on profit-making (paid) events. Conference and retreat centers may be available for daylong workshops.

As you call and visit possible locations for your workshop, find out what kinds of chairs and tables they have, what audiovisual equipment is available, and what the arrangements would be for beverage and snacks. If you use church or school facilities, you will probably be able to bring your own coffeepot and snacks as long as you clean up afterward. Hotels and some conference centers charge a hefty fee for coffee and snack service, and they do not allow you to bring in any food from the outside. Especially in dealing with hotels, make sure you are clear about all the charges. If you ask whether they have a projection screen, they may say, "Sure, we can provide that." You must ascertain whether or not there will be an extra charge for audiovisual rental. They will not necessarily volunteer this information. You must know to ask.

❏ BASICS OF WORKSHOP FINANCES AND PRICING

The main sources of revenue for most workshops are the registration fees paid by participants, but additional revenues may come from sales of books, manuals, tapes, CDs, videos, newsletter subscriptions, and other products; display fees paid by organizations who want to set up a booth or table to promote their products or services; and contributions from sponsors who donate to help make the workshop possible or to provide scholarships for participants. Most leader-sponsored workshops have revenue only from registration fees and sales of "back of the room" books and tapes (so named because they are usually set up for sale at the back of the room).

To determine your profit (or loss), you add up the revenues and subtract the expenses. Remember that before the workshop takes place, you can only project what the revenues and expenses will be. A critical factor in determining your expenses is deciding how much your time is worth. At a minimum, you should consider the hours spent leading the workshop as an expense at your usual hourly rate. In addition, you need to account for the hours spent planning and preparing the workshop.

Here is an example for a 1-day workshop (to make it simple, we will assume that people pay for their own lunch). All of the charges are to be taken only as examples and may not be representative of the charges you will incur:

TABLE 10.1 COST OF A 1-DAY WORKSHOP

Revenue:

Workshop registrations: 20 people at $125 each = $2,500

Expenses:

Your time of 8 hours at $90/hour	$720
Conference center rental	$300
Layout and printing of 2,200 flyers	$300
Mailing 2,000 flyers	$750
Small ads in 2 professional newsletters	$100
Workshop handouts (printing, pocket folders)	$100
Drinks and snacks at registration and breaks	$50
Total Expenses:	$2,320
Net Profit (or Loss)	$180

Using the same example, if only 15 people had registered, the revenue would have been $1,875, with a resulting loss of $445. On the other hand, if 30 people attended, the revenue would have been $3,750 causing only a small increase in the cost of handouts and snacks, with a profit of almost $1,430.

If the workshop fee had been set at $85 per person, the revenue from 20 people would have been $1,700, for a loss of $620. If only 15 people signed up at $85, the revenue would have been $1,275, resulting in a $1,045 loss. With 30 people registering at $85 each, the income would have been $2,550 for a $230 profit.

In these examples, we have not factored in the leader's time spent preparing for the workshop. If we did, all of the above examples would have resulted in a loss, although the leader may not pay out more than he or she received in revenue. You may decide that you receive other "value" besides the income from the workshop, such as new clients, more consulting business, exposure in the community, and the opportunity to develop future revenue from products such as workbooks, tapes, videos, and so on. The time you spend designing the first workshop may be viewed as an investment for future workshops that will take much less time to prepare. The point is not that you must be directly compensated for your time in cash revenue, but that your time is a cost since the time you spend preparing and leading the workshop takes away time that you could use for another, possibly revenue-producing, activity.

In deciding on a registration fee for your workshop, study what other seminars of the same type and length are charging. Describe the workshop to people who fit your participant profile and ask them what range they would expect to pay. Do not set the registration fees too low. You do not want to set them too high either, but many therapists, and some coaches, have issues with charging what they are worth, so get input from other knowledgeable professionals. With a higher fee, you may have room to offer a discount for early registration or to offer partial scholarships for students. Set up a spreadsheet similar to the one above, with your projected expenses, and see what different fees and attendance numbers would leave as profit.

Market and promote more than you think is necessary. As you can see from the examples, getting 10 more registrants makes a big difference in the profit. The way to get more people is to market it well. That means designing a topic and a flyer that attract people, mailing to as large a list as you can afford, getting all the mailings out at least 8 weeks before the event, and doing follow-up publicity as you get closer to the date.

❏ DESIGNING AND LEADING AN EFFECTIVE WORKSHOP

What are the keys to designing an effective workshop or seminar? Although there are certainly differences in approach and content between an hour-long workshop for parents of teenagers on how to set boundaries and a daylong workshop for psychologists on changes in diagnostic criteria, successful workshops of such different audiences and focus have more similarities than differences.

Characteristics of Adult Learners

To design effective workshops, you need to keep in mind how adults learn and how they want to learn. Adults generally want:

- To have input into what and how they learn.
- To integrate what they are learning with what they already know.
- To have a learning environment that is active, experiential, and interactive.
- To have learning to be practical and applicable to real life.
- To have learning processes to enhance their self-esteem.
- To have learning processes to allow social interaction as well as individual exploration.

Essential Tips for Making the Workshop Effective

Near the beginning of the workshop, ask about participants' experience and background, their reasons for taking the workshop, and what they want to learn. Get people talking to one another early in the workshop so they begin to feel a connection and a sense of belonging. Provide name tags to make it easier for people to connect with one another (and for you to remember their names).

Provide a clear organization and structure for the workshop, including clear learning objectives. Tell people your agenda, but be willing to adjust time frames and emphases to better meet their needs. Make sure people can ask questions and give input all along the way, not just at the end. Keep the agenda moving so you can include the key points the workshop was designed to cover. Let people know regularly where you are in the agenda.

Plan for different levels of previous experience and knowledge so that beginners are not lost and more experienced people are not bored. One way is to plan alternative activities for more or less experienced people, or to group people according to their experience level. When you present theory or research, link it to real-life applications and to their own practice.

Find ways to present content without long lectures and to make the learning active, experiential, and interactive. Examples include:

- Ice breakers

- Sharing in pairs, triads, and small groups
- Role plays
- Small group exercises
- Competitions between groups
- Team presentations
- Discussion
- Brainstorming
- Games
- Videos
- Case studies
- Quizzes, tests, and self-assessments

Plan safe and incremental ways for participants to share and practice what they are learning in the workshop setting. Do not ask questions that put people on the spot, make them wrong, or embarrass them. Give people opportunities to learn from one another as well as from you.

Allow adequate time for breaks (restroom breaks, getting drinks and snacks, stretching and moving around). If possible, give people a chance to get outside sometime during the day. Plan exercises so that everyone has an opportunity to interact with several other people during the workshop.

Include ways for participants to reflect on what they learned during the workshop and to develop steps for applying the learning afterward. Suggest ways they can get support for ongoing application of the learning. Allow time at the end for people to complete feedback sheets.

❏ TELECLASSES AND TELESEMINARS

Teleclasses, teleseminars, and teleconferences are a relatively recent but growing direction for workshops and seminars, with coaches being one of the biggest users. These terms usually refer to classes held entirely by telephone, with all participants calling a central "bridge line" telephone number that allows all participants to listen and talk on the same call. The bridge numbers will be long distance for most callers, but at today's rates, that is seldom a problem. Although it is possible to arrange for a toll-free bridge line, you must pay a substantial premium for each person on the call (at least 15 cents per minute per person), so this is rarely practical outside of corporate teleseminars.

Most teleclasses last 60 to 90 minutes. They may be individual events or part of a series, typically weekly, that lasts for 2 to 8 sessions. Many coaches offer an initial free teleclass for the same reasons they may offer free in-person workshops—as a way to share a topic they are passionate about, to become known, to sell books or tapes, and to develop relationships with people who might be interested in retaining a coach. Dave Buck, a professional coach and now head of CoachVille.com, started his coaching practice by offering a free tele-seminar every week for a year. In less than a year, he had a full practice as well as many other speaking and training opportunities, without doing any other marketing beyond the teleseminars and his Web site.

Increasingly, teleclasses are also being offered, for fees ranging from \$19 to \$49 per session.

How to Get Started with Teleclasses

If you have never participated in a teleclass before, start by signing up for some free teleclasses to see what they are like and to see how leaders handle the discussion. You can find free teleclasses by doing a Web search for "free teleclass" or by going to any of the following teleseminar Web sites:

- www.teleclass.com
- www.teleclass4u.com
- www.teleclassinternational.com

If you decide you would like to try leading teleclasses, consider signing up for a teleclass on how to lead teleclasses. Most of the main teleclass listing sites offer teleclass leader training, and many of them require that you take it before you can list your teleclass with their site. As part of the training, you will start designing your own teleseminar.

Whether or not you decide you're ready to offer your own tele-classes, you may want to consider offering to be a guest speaker on a teleconference hosted by someone else. Your expertise or specialty as a coach (or therapist) could make you an ideal guest for a teleconference sponsored by a coach with a different specialty. For example, if you are a career coach, you could be a guest on a teleconference led by a relationship coach on how work and career affects relationships. If you are a business coach, you could be a guest on a teleconference for life coaches on paying attention to the business side of coaching. If you are a therapist, you could be a guest talking with other coaches about how to know when a client needs more help than coaching can offer.

Why would you want to volunteer to be a guest on someone else's teleconference? You will get experience, you'll receive exposure from the publicity sent out to sign up people, you can refer participants to your Web site and offer them subscriptions to your e-zine, and if you have a book or tape to sell, you can give your buying information to the participants. As with traditional speaking, the more people hear about you, the more likely you are to be offered other opportunities to speak.

How can you arrange guest appearances on others' teleconferences? Decide on a few topics that you have something to say and enjoy talking about. Ask coaches you meet if they know of teleconferences that might be interested in having you as a guest. Do Web searches "coaching teleconference" and look for possible matches among those you find. Call or e-mail other coaches asking if they would be interested in you bring a guest on a teleconference. Tell them briefly about the expertise you being and the benefits for their guests. If you follow these steps, you will likely have all the guest invitations you want within a few months.

Setting Up Your Own Teleseminar

Teleseminars are one of the easiest types of presentations to arrange because you do not have to find a place to meet and you are not limited by geographical distance. You will probably hear participants from

Great Britain, Australia, and New Zealand on some of the teleclasses you sign up for. Here are the steps to take:

1. Decide on a topic for a teleseminar you want to offer. In the beginning you will probably start by offering a 1 hour teleclass, so choose a topic you can cover in 1 hour. Some people offer a 1-hour free teleclass as an introduction to a longer teleclass series that people pay for.

2. Plan the basic outline of one to five key points. Most teleclasses are very interactive, so do not overload the outline with content. Plan to present your material in short bite-sized nuggets and let handouts cover more of the details. Design your outline to draw strongly on participants' experience, answers, ideas, concerns, and questions.

3. Reserve a bridge line for the time and date of your seminar. Bridge lines can be rented by the hour through the teleclass Web sites mentioned earlier and other sources for $10 or $15 per hour. You can get packages of hours for even less. You can find many providers by doing a Web search for "telephone bridge" or "telephone conferencing."

4. Publicize your teleclass through your own e-mail lists as well as one of the teleclass sites. These sites charge a fee for listing your teleclass, but some of the most popular sites get thousands of people looking at the listings. The sites also handle the entire registration process and provide you with a list of participants, including e-mail addresses.

5. Send out greeting and reminder e-mails to participants, including any handouts you want them to have in advance. Many teleclass leaders structure the workshop so they send out the handouts afterward.

6. Be prepared well in advance of the time to begin so you can call in to the bridge line and get off to a positive start.

7. Enjoy the process.

WORKSHEET 10.1. Speaker and Workshop Checklist

Use this checklist to create your own list for remembering what to pack
for a speaking engagement or workshop.

___ Directions to location

___ Name and phone number of contact person

___ Presentation notes

___ Registration roster

___ Continuing education certificates

___ Name tags

___ Name tent cards

___ Extra paper

___ Pens and pencils

___ Notecards

___ Masking tape

___ Stapler

___ Paper clips

___ Flip chart stands and pads

___ Handouts in folders or binders

___ Thumb tacks

___ Chalk

___ Markers in various colors for writing on flip chart

___ White board markers

___ Overhead projector with spare bulb

___ VCR player

___ Videotapes

___ Extension cords and/or power strip

___ Duct tape (to tape over extension cords)

___ Transparencies (including blanks)

___ Transparency markers

___ Laptop computer

___ Printer

___ LCD projector

___ Cables for projector

___ Camcorder with tripod

___ Tapes for camcorder

___ Recording device and microphone

___ Extra batteries for above

___ Books or tapes to sell

___ Money to make change

___ Credit card supplies

___ Bottled water

___ Sugar-free throat lozenges

___ Pain reliever for headache

___ Band-Aids

CHAPTER 11

Improving Academic
and Medical Presentations

ACADEMIC OR MEDICAL PRESENTATIONS present some unique challenges quite different from presentations to community, business, or consumer groups. In this chapter we will discuss some of the special types of academic and medical presentations, besides class lectures, and how to handle them effectively. We will look at the common mistakes that presenters make in academic and medical settings and how you can make your presentations interesting and memorable instead of dry and forgettable. Rather than repeating the phrase "academic and medical presentations" throughout, you can assume that in this chapter the terms *presentations* and *presenters* refer to academic and medical settings.

The special presentations that psychologists, psychiatrists, social workers, counselors, clinical nurse specialists, and marriage and family therapists often give in academic and medical settings include presentations to colleagues and professional students in related disciplines (including grand rounds), paper presentations within an institution and at conferences, and panel presentations and discussions. Psychiatrists often speak to groups of medical students, residents, nurses, physician's assistants, psychologists, and social workers. All of the disciplines bring their own research and expertise that they may present to many of these other related health-care providers.

❑ PRESENTING A PAPER

One of the unique and particularly challenging presentations is the presenting of a paper. The paper is a scholarly, research-based article that is to be published. In some settings, it is expected that the paper will be read at the presentation, almost word for word. In other contexts, the presentation is a summary and explanation of the research described in the paper but is not expected to be a reading of the paper itself. We include both kinds of paper presentations in the suggestions that follow.

The 10 most common mistakes that undermine presentation effectiveness are that speakers:

1. Write their presentations without considering the special needs of a "listening" audience as compared to a "reading" audience.
2. Use specialized terminology or acronyms without defining and explaining the terms.
3. Overwhelm their audiences with numbers, statistics, or other details.
4. Read the entire presentation with little or no eye contact with their audience.
5. Speak in a monotone voice or with vocalized pauses that distract the audience.
6. Talk too fast for the audience to take in their meaning or too slow for the audience to maintain interest.
7. Read word for word from their PowerPoint slides.
8. Keep the audience past time because they do not keep track of the time.
9. Present theories or research without connecting the material to a human element or its effects on people.
10. Do not reveal their own interest, engagement, or passion about the topic.

Fortunately, these problems can be solved fairly easily.

The first three presentation mistakes can be viewed as problems with the writing or the way the content is constructed. Presentation Mistakes 4 through 8 can be seen as problems with delivery. Presentation Mistakes 9 and 10 are about underestimating the human aspect of presenting.

Overcoming Writing Problems

If you make any of the first three mistakes, what can you do to eliminate these problems?

First, you can write for listeners as well as readers. Make the structure of your talk explicit and clear. Tell them what you are going to tell them. Tell them. Then tell them what you told them. Summarize or recap often. Tell them when you are moving to a new point. Make your transitions explicit. Otherwise, if listeners' attention lapses for a few seconds, they may be lost.

When presenting a paper, do a version that will make it easier for you and the audience to follow in the spoken format. To make it easier for you to follow, print out a version in a larger font (14 or 16 point). Mark it up by underlining key words, putting in slash marks where you want to pause, and adding reminders in the margins such as SMILE, LOOK UP, and VOCAL VARIETY.

To make it easier for the audience to follow, avoid complex sentences whose meaning is unclear until the end. For example: "In our research, which was conducted over the course of 2 years using a series of double-blind studies, we found, despite our initial expectations, that the efficacy of medication alone was not validated." This sentence might be acceptable in an article, but not in a speech. The complete meaning of the sentence is not known until the last two words. This example might be revised to say: "We conducted a series of double-blind studies over 2 years. The efficacy of medication alone was not validated, despite our initial expectations to the contrary."

As part of your editing and revising process, read your paper aloud, listening for words, phrases, and constructions that are awkward or hard to understand on first hearing. Even better, read it to a friend or colleague to see which parts they have trouble understanding. As with any writing, use active voice and simple words whenever possible. Edit out unnecessary words and phrases. Consult an English usage guide to help you spot wordiness.

Whenever you use specialized terminology or acronyms, define the term or abbreviation the first time you use it. If you will be speaking to an audience with significantly different levels of knowledge or experience with the topic, give explanations for anything that some audience members may not know. For example, if you are doing a presentation on depression to an audience of all psychiatrists or psychologists, you would not need to define the term or list the common symptoms. But if you are speaking to a group that includes family physicians, nurses, or physicians assistants, you should briefly list the symptoms of depression, especially the less obvious ones.

If you are not sure how much your audience knows about a particular subject, ask if anyone would like you to explain it in more detail. If you were talking about anxiety disorders, you could say: "Would anyone like me to do a quick overview of the diagnostic differences between panic disorder and generalized anxiety disorder?" Do not ask, "Is there anyone here who doesn't know the differences?" Some people are reluctant to admit that they do not know something, but they are more willing to say if they would like more explanation. If one person requests the overview, explain it to the group. Others will also appreciate the explanation.

Numbers and statistics are an essential part of many academic and medical presentations, but the human mind can only absorb so many statistics in one sitting. What can you do to avoid the mistake of overwhelming your audience with numbers? Choose the most important data and highlight it. You may include the rest of the numbers in your paper or PowerPoint, but tell your audience what to focus on. Summarize the rest rather than going over everything in detail. Spend time designing your charts and graphs to make them quickly understandable. Label the columns or axes clearly, using fonts that are large enough to read. Translate key numbers into comparisons and analogies. For example, instead of just stating that about 4 million people in the United States suffer from panic disorder, tell them this is the equivalent of the entire population of Atlanta and its suburbs.

In presenting research, plan the most interesting, engaging, and efficient method for telling your story. The best way is usually not to tell them the history of the project in a step-by-step, detailed linear story. "First we did this and then we did that" can quickly bore an audience. Instead, start with the question your research was designed to answer, and make it as intriguing as possible. Make your audience want to know what you discovered. Summarize the methodology without all the blow-by-blow details. Focus much of your time on your findings and conclusions. Be sure to allow time for questions.

Overcoming Delivery Problems

If you make any of Presentation Mistakes 4 through 8, how can you correct them?

If you are not sure whether you speak with a monotone, record yourself and listen for how much variety you use in your voice as well as whether you are speaking faster or slower than speakers you enjoy. Ask a friend or colleague to listen to the tape and give suggestions about how you can add interest and variety in your voice. Practice by varying your pitch, pace, and volume. Make the variety fit what you are saying. Emphasize key words. Pause to add impact and to allow time for people to take in what you have said. Increase or lower your volume slightly to draw attention to key words or phrases.

Consider the following statements as an example: "Study after study has shown that the most effective treatment for depression is a combination of medication and psychotherapy. Does this mean that every single patient should be given medication and receive psychotherapy? No. The studies show that statistically more patients report improvement from a combination of medication and psychotherapy. Some patients only need medication. Other patients need only psychotherapy. But most patients do better when they receive both." If read monotonously, without emphasis, these words could give audiences reason to tune out.

Instead, here's an example of how to make the same words more interesting and easier for the listener to understand (I have shown emphasis by underlining and indicated pauses in parentheses):

> Study after study has shown that the <u>most effective</u> treatment for <u>depression</u> is a <u>combination</u> of medication and psychotherapy. (Pause) Does this mean that <u>every single patient</u> should be given medication <u>and</u> receive psychotherapy? (Slight pause) <u>No</u>. (Pause) The studies show that <u>statistically</u> more patients report improvement from a <u>combination</u> of medication and psychotherapy. <u>Some</u> patients only need <u>medication</u>. Other patients need <u>only</u> psychotherapy. (Slight pause) But <u>most</u> patients do better when they receive <u>both</u>.

If adding variety and emphasis seems foreign to you, first read portions of your own material without adding emphasis. Then read them again as though you were reading it as a story to a child, making the meaning clear by how you read it. Try exaggerating the variety in your practice until you feel more comfortable with it.

If you have trouble making eye contact, do the following: If you are reading a paper, practice seeing a whole phrase each time you look down, so you can look up and say most of the phrase before looking back down for what comes next. Of course, the more you practice, the better you will know and remember your key points and phrases. Slide a finger along the text as you speak so that you will be able to find your place easily after looking up at the audience. A rule of thumb, or at least a guideline, is that you should only be speaking when you are looking out at your audience.

One way to make eye contact with different parts of the audience is to think of your audience as having four sections (near right, near left, far right, far left). As you speak, make eye contact in a series of crisscross patterns, starting with near right, then far left, then far right, then near left, and then repeating the pattern. Look at a different person each time. If possible, maintain your eye contact with a person for the length of a phrase or sentence rather than darting from person to person. The purpose of eye contact is to make a connection with members of your audience and draw them in. Rapidly shifting eye contact can make you seem nervous or uninterested in connecting.

If you use PowerPoint, you will probably be tempted to read the slides to your audience. After all, you put what you wanted to say on those slides. Overcome the temptation. Use the slides to complement and enhance your presentation, but do not consider them to be your presentation and do not use them as your script. When you move to a new slide, pause briefly to give the audience time to read the content. Then summarize or make the point in a different way. If the slide is easy to understand, you may proceed as though the words on the slide have already been said. You can go on to explain and elaborate what the slide is about. One caution: If there is any chance that not everyone can see the slides well enough to read them or if the lecture is being audio-taped, then summarize the slide's message. For more tips on using PowerPoint effectively, review the suggestions in Chapter 6.

Predicting the length of a presentation and keeping track of time is difficult for many speakers. Even if you carefully time your presentation in practice, you cannot anticipate delayed starting times, audiovisual technical problems, or the amount of audience discussion. Your own excitement and reaction to the audience may also change your pace from when you practiced. As a guideline, plan your presentation to use only 75% of the time you expect to have. If you expect to have a total of 60 minutes for your presentation, prepare a presentation that you can give in about 45 minutes when you practice. That will provide a cushion for starting late, technical problems, audience participation, and your adding comments as you speak. Finishing with a few minutes to spare is far better than cramming at the end or having people starting to leave, mentally or actually, while you are concluding.

Bringing in the Human Element

What presentations have you heard that you remember? Besides those by famous or brilliant presenters, the presentations you remember are probably those that vividly brought the human element to life. They probably described real people in ways that made them live, made you feel you knew them or wanted to know them. Perhaps you identified with their struggles, admired their persistence, relished their successes, or were saddened by their losses.

How can you connect with the human in your presentations? Along with whatever else you present, talk about one or more real people. Introduce them.

William Meyer, a clinical social worker and engaging presenter, says you have to find a way to tell a story. "What people are hungry for and what they remember are stories," he says. There is a story behind every theory, every research project, and every psychiatric disorder and treatment. When presenting a developmental model or therapeutic approach, he finds that audiences are often more receptive if they hear something about the people who developed a model or therapy. What in their lives helped form their perspectives? What was their relationship with other practitioners? What were their dreams and struggles? The human interest side of a theory or a project can give listeners reasons to remember, to relate, and to want to know even more.

If you are describing a patient, do not simply give the typical medical data of age, race, marital status, and occupation. Use the novelist's tools of description and characterization. Here is a typical patient description:

> Robert was a 36-year-old Caucasian male, divorced, recently unemployed as a middle-level manager who presented with a history of compulsive gambling.

Here is an example of bringing in the human:

> The first time I saw Robert, he was nervously leafing through the waiting room magazines as though desperately searching for something in the pages. Perhaps he was, because as I soon learned, this 36-year-old man had lost everything—his wife, his family, his house, his savings, and now his job, because he gambled compulsively on everything from horses to hockey—

anything with a winner and a loser. I still remember the irony of his words that day: "I decided to take a chance on coming here. I know it's a long shot, but I'm about out of chances." At that time he saw all of life as a crap shoot, and an important part of our work together would be to help him find places where he could feel some control without resorting to the magical thinking of the gambler.

❑ PARTICIPATING IN PANEL DISCUSSIONS

A common form of presentation in academic and medical settings is the panel discussion. These vary considerably in format, but typically three or more panelists give presentations of a prescribed length, with questions and discussion from the audience at the end. A moderator usually introduces the topic and guides the discussion.

If You Are the Moderator

You can improve the likelihood of a good panel discussion if you contact the panelists well in advance, telling them all the details of the event, especially what their topic is, how long their presentation is to be, who the other panelists and their topics will be, when and where to meet before the event, and how they can contact you if they have questions. Be very clear about the maximum time they will have to speak and emphasize the importance of honoring the time limit. The most common problem with panels happens when panelists speak far longer than their allotted time, knocking the entire schedule askew.

Ask the panelists to confirm their receiving your information and, if possible, call or e-mail them to discuss any questions they may have. Do not assume that a lack of response means they have no questions. They may have simply forgotten it or missed your e-mail.

Meet with the panelists a few minutes prior to the panel discussion to go over the arrangements and the flow for the event. Arrange for a timer to signal the panelists about their remaining time, starting when they have 2 minutes remaining. Be prepared to interrupt panelists politely but firmly if they go over their time limit by more than 2 minutes.

When you introduce the panel and the discussion, explain the flow to the audience, especially if you want them to save their questions until all panelists have spoken or if you want them to write out their questions on cards and submit them to you. Receiving the questions in written form can be a good way to avoid speechmaking from the audience. This also lets you combine similar questions and rephrase them for clarity.

Your role as moderator is usually to make the discussion go smoothly, not to make a presentation yourself. Unless you are also presenting, avoid the temptation to make your own speech. You can be most effective in introducing the topic and the panelists briefly, guiding the discussion, keeping it going, and summarizing it at the end.

If You Are a Panelist

If your moderator follows the guidelines outlined here, you will know clearly what is expected of you. If not, ask. Contact the moderator or coordinator to find out the details, especially the topic and time frames you should follow. Allow plenty of time to arrive early, especially if you are unfamiliar with the location.

Clarify with the moderator the order of speaking and whether you are to take questions or defer them to the end. Introduce yourself to the other panelists if they are unknown to you.

During your panel presentation, avoid long preambles and get to the point. If no provision has been made for time signals, ask someone to signal you when 1 or 2 minutes remain of your time, or set your own watch so you will know when your time is up.

While other panelists are speaking, listen. Even though you are not "on," the audience will see and notice your actions. If you fidget or look restlessly around the room, you may be viewed as bored or even rude.

In the discussion after the presentations, be courteous. If you disagree strongly with what others have said, say so, but avoid attacking or embarrassing them. You may end up being the one who is embarrassed.

The essence of good academic and medical presentations is content communicated. Content alone is not enough, no matter how brilliant. When good content is communicated and presented effectively, the content that would otherwise be overlooked or ignored comes alive in the listeners' minds. When your ideas or research or teaching take root in others' minds because you planted them (presented them) well, the whole endeavor fulfills its purpose. The process of planting and presenting ideas is one we are always learning. It is always worth learning to do well.

Resources

❏ BOOKS

Adubato, Steve. (2002). *Speak from the heart: Be yourself and get results.* New York: The Free Press. An Emmy award-winning broadcaster gives many helpful suggestions for communicating from the inside out.

Ailes, Roger. (1995). *You are the message: Getting what you want by being who you are.* New York: Doubleday. A longtime speech coach to presidents and celebrities tells the reader what he tells his clients.

Berckhan, B., Krause, C., & Roeder, U. (2000). *Public and professional speaking: A confident approach for women.* London: Free Association Books. This guide is helpful to men as well as women, with its focus on developing the ability to feel at ease and to speak with confidence.

Bly, R. (2001). Getting *started in speaking, training, or seminar consulting.* New York: Wiley. The author gives a helpful overview of the field and includes good examples of promotional materials.

Bly, R. (2002). *Become a recognized authority in your field in 60 days or less!* Indianapolis, IN: Alpha Books. Despite the title, this guide contains helpful chapters on speaking, seminars, and e-zines.

Bridges, W. (1980). *Transitions.* New York: Addison-Wesley.

Burns, D. D. (1999). *Feeling good: The new mood therapy.* New York: Avon.

Campbell, G. M. (2002). *Bullet proof presentations.* Franklin Lakes, NJ: Career Press. The first half of this book gives helpful suggestions on how to develop the content of your presentation.

Franklin, R. A. (1996). *The consultant's guide to publicity: How to make a name for yourself by promoting your expertise.* New York: Wiley. Although written for consultants, the information applies to therapists and coaches too.

Friedman, R. J., & Altman, P. (1997) *How to design, develop, and market health care seminars.* Sarasota, FL: Professional Resource Press. This nuts-and-bolts guide is an excellent resource for those wanting to produce their own seminars.

Gallo, F. P., & Vincenzi, H. (2000). *Energy tapping.* Oakland, CA: New Harbinger Publications. This guide teaches the reader how to use acupressure points to relieve anxiety.

Gendlin, E. (1982). *Focusing.* New York: Bantam Books. This classic describes an invaluable process for giving words and voice to what is often hard to describe in our experience.

Glickstein, L. (1998). *Be heard now.* New York: Bantam Books. The author founded "Speaking Circles" to deal with his own stage fright and has helped thousands using the methods outlined in this book.

Grand, L. C. (2000a). *The life skills presentation guide.* New York: Wiley. The author is a therapist and instructional designer. She gives excellent detailed outlines for workshops and presentations that you can adapt for your own use.

Grand, L. C. (2000b). *The marriage and family presentation guide.* New York: Wiley. This volume contains outlines for workshops and presentations on marriage and family topics.

Hayden, C. J. (1999). *Get clients now: A 28-day marketing program for professionals and consultants.* New York: AMACOM. An excellent guide to marketing professional services.

Hoff, R. (1992). *I can see you naked (rev. ed.).* Kansas City, MO: Andrews and McMeel. A classic guide to public speaking that is filled with helpful tips.

Holliday, M. (2000). *Secrets of power presentations (2nd ed.).* Franklin Lakes, NJ: Career Press. The author trains seminar leaders and professional speakers. This guide is almost as good as taking her class.

Jeary, T. (2004). *Life is a series of presentations.* New York: Simon & Schuster. This excellent book by an executive presentations coach is filled with practical advice you can apply in all your interactions.

Jolles, R. L. (1993). *How to run seminars and workshops: Presentation skills for consultants, trainers, and teachers.* New York: Wiley. Another excellent guide that focuses on leading workshops and seminars.

Katie, B. (2002). *Loving what is: Four questions that can change your life.* New York: Harmony Books. Details the author's approach to challenging self-defeating thinking.

Kushner, M. (1997). *Successful presentations for dummies.* Foster City, CA: IDG Books. A comprehensive guide to every aspect of public speaking and presenting.

Maguire, J. (1998). *The power of personal storytelling: Spinning tales to connect with others.* New York: Jeremy P. Tarcher/Putnam. This is the best guide I have seen on how to tell personal stories effectively.

Maisel, E. (1997). *Fearless presenting.* New York: Back Stage Books. The author is a psychologist specializing in creative artists and performers. In this book he outlines many approaches to dealing with your fear of presenting.

Nice, S. E. (1999). *Speaking for impact: Connecting with every audience.* Boston: Allyn and Bacon. As the title suggests, this book focuses on ways to develop rapport with your audience.

Peoples, D. A. (1992). *Presentations plus: David People's proven techniques (rev. ed.).* New York: Wiley. A classic presentation guide with lots of practical tips.

Pinskey, R. (1997). *101 ways to promote yourself.* New York: Avon Books. Packed with specific practical ideas for getting publicity.

Rogers, N. H. (2000). *The new talk power: The mind-body way to speak without fear.* Sterling, VA: Capital Books. The author is a clinical social worker and former actress who specializes in helping people overcome their fear of public speaking.

Sarnoff, D. (1997). *Never be nervous again.* New York: Fawcett Books. This book by a veteran speaking coach contains good public speaking advice on much more than dealing with nervousness.

Shenson, H. (1990). *How to develop and promote successful seminars and workshops.* New York: Wiley. A practical guide to producing workshops and seminars.

Silber, L. (2001). *Self-promotion for the creative person.* New York: Random House. This book is based on the author's interviews with many artists and musicians, and includes excellent ideas for self-promotion that you will not find elsewhere.

Slutsky, J., & Aun, M. (1997). *The toastmasters international guide to successful speaking.* Chicago: Dearborn Financial Publishing. This is the basic Toastmasters guide and includes lots of good suggestions for putting together your presentation.

Van Yoder, S. (2003). *Get slightly famous.* Berkeley, CA: Bay Tree Publishing. A guide to using a variety of methods, including public speaking, for building a reputation.

Walters, D., & Walters, L. (2002). *Speak and grow rich (rev. and updated ed.).* Paramus, NJ: Prentice Hall. This is an excellent behind-the-scenes guide on how to make money as a public speaker.

Weiss, A. (1998). *Money talks: How to make a million as a speaker.* New York: McGraw-Hill. The author is a consultant as well as a popular speaker with excellent advice for coaches and psychotherapists on how to get paid for speaking.

Wilder, C. (1994). *The presentations kit: 10 steps for selling your ideas (rev. and updated ed.).* New York: Wiley. Although geared to business presentations, this book is a goldmine of checklists and practical suggestions for organizing your presentations.

Wilder, L. (1999). *7 steps to fearless speaking.* New York: Wiley. The author has coached thousands of broadcasters and celebrities, including Oprah. If I could only buy one other book on public speaking, this would probably be the one.

Yudkin, M. (2003). *6 steps to free publicity, rev. ed.* Franklin Lakes, NJ: Career Press. This is an excellent practical guide to getting publicity for whatever you do.

❏ REFERENCE BOOKS

These are usually available in your public or university library reference section.

Bacon's Newspaper/Magazine Directory. Lists every newspaper and periodical with contact information, including a geographical index. A good reference for developing your own local publicity mailing list.

Chase's Calendar of Events: The Day-by-Day Directory to Special Days, Weeks, and Months. Lists thousands of special days, weeks, and months that you can use to get publicity.

Encyclopedia of Associations. Comprehensive listing of thousands of associations listed by name and topic. An excellent resource for finding conferences where you might speak.

Standard Rate and Data Service. Includes descriptions of mailing lists that are available. A good place to look if you are considering offering a specialty workshop or seminar.

❏ ORGANIZATIONS

American Society for Training and Development (ASTD)
1640 King St.
P. O. Box 1443
Alexandria, VA 22313
(703) 683-8100
www.astd.org

Dale Carnegie Training
www.dalecarnegie.com

National Speakers Association
1500 S. Priest Drive
Tempe, AZ 85281
www.nsaspeaker.org
(480) 968-2552

Speaking Circles International
P.O. Box 674
Woodacre, CA 94973-0674
(415) 488-4460
(800) 610-0169
www.speakingcircles.com

Toastmasters International
P.O. Box 9052
Mission Viejo, CA 92690
www.toastmasters.org
(949) 858-8255

❏ INTERNET

Marketing and Publicity Resources

www.actionplan.com—Robert Middleton, a marketing coach, offers an excellent free Marketing Plan Workbook at his site.

www.internetprguide.com—Extensive articles on how to get publicity for your practice.

www.prweb.com—Internet news release distribution service that includes tips for preparing an effective news release.

www.publicityinsider.com—Free newsletter and reports from a veteran publicity expert.

Speaking Resources

www.emofree.com—This site provides resources on the emotional freedom technique (EFT), a helpful tool for reducing anxiety and stage fright.

www.focusing.org—An excellent resource for those who want to learn to speak from a deeper place.

www.fripp.com—Patricia Fripp is an award-winning speaker and
   speaking coach with many free resources available at her site.
www.greatvoice.com—Free newsletter and tips for improving your
   voice by a professional voice coach.
www.joyfulmarketing.com —Laura Howard, a workshop coach, offers
   a free Workshop Design Guide downloadable at her site.
www.nsaspeaker.org—The National Speakers Association has an excellent "knowledge base" of articles that anyone can access.
www.public-speaking.org—Extensive collection of free speaking tips.
www.sullivanspeaker.com—Vickie Sullivan coaches professional
   speakers but includes several free reports for speakers on her Web
   site.

Seminar Resources

Because seminar companies change frequently, I recommend you find
current resources by doing an online Google or Yahoo search for "seminars for mental health professionals" or "seminars for personal
coaches."

Teleclass Resources

www.freeconferencing.com
www.telebridge.com
www.teleclass.com
www.teleclass4u.com
www.teleclassinternational.com

❏ TO CONTACT THE AUTHOR

Dan Grandstaff
(919) 968-2122
dan@winwithpeople.com

Index